Praise for

101 Ways to Say Thank You

"This book is an indispensable resource for our young adults learning not only the power of a thank-you note but also the essential need of practicing everyday civility and global respect in our digital world. They need to know the power of people skills!"

—*Pamela Eyring, owner and president of The Protocol School of Washington*

"Practicing gratefulness is essential to your happiness and success, no matter how old you are! *101 Ways to Say Thank You: Kids & Teens* will help you honor the tradition of the classic thank-you note while embracing the digital revolution with grace and style. Around the block or around the globe, good manners will take you where you want to go!"

—*Debra Lassiter, Cindy Haygood & April McLean, The Etiquette & Leadership Institute*

101 Ways to Say Thank You!

Thank You!

xo

All-Occasion Thank-You Note Templates,
Social Media Etiquette & Gratitude Guide
for Kids & Teens

Kelly Browne

Plain Sight Publishing
An Imprint of Cedar Fort, Inc.
Springville, Utah

ISBN 13: 978-1-4621-1641-6

Published by Plain Sight Publishing,
An imprint of Cedar Fort, Inc.
2373 W. 700 S., Springville, UT 84663

Distributed by Cedar Fort, Inc., www.cedarfort.com

LIBRARY OF CONGRESS CATALOGING-IN-PUBLICATION DATA
Browne, Kelly, 1966- author.
101 ways to say thank you for kids and teens / Kelly Browne.
pages cm
Includes bibliographical references.
ISBN 978-1-4621-1641-6 (alk. paper)
1. Thank-you notes. 2. Etiquette for children and teenagers. I. Title. II. Title: One hundred and one ways to say thank you for kids and teens.

BJ2115.T45B76 2015
395.4--dc23

2015008364

Cover design by Jen Niepraschk
Cover design © 2015 by Lyle Mortimer
Edited by Eileen Leavitt
Typeset by Angela Decker

Printed in the United States of America

10 9 8 7 6 5 4 3 2 1

Printed on acid-free paper

To my gorgeous, gracious girls, Greta and Ava Browne,
and grateful guys, my nephews, Mick Kerrigan and William Burrier.

A portion of the author's royalties have been donated to children's charities.

Contents

Foreword

In today's world of quick emails, texts, and video chats, the handwritten thank-you note always makes the best impression and remains a powerful tool for success in every area of your life. While the honored tradition of pen and paper rule, times are changing, and we can embrace the many ways to express our thanks, show our gratitude, and promote respect online. With social media at our fingertips, remember that we are citizens of the world, and it is important to practice everyday civility in all we say and do—online or off—to leave a positive digital imprint that reflects the person we want the world to see.

Kelly Browne's modern thank-you notes are an invaluable resource for every gift and significant occasion in a young person's life—from birthdays to spiritual milestones. She also includes information on how to address athletic teams, teachers, interview participants, and holiday celebration organizers, and how to simply be grateful for the wonderful support and love of family and friends. Here you will find straightforward tips and tricks to provide our young adults with the guidance they need to quickly write their notes and to navigate the ever more challenging social pitfalls of cyberspace with grace, dignity, and style.

As our world embraces the digital revolution, the virtues of gratitude and civility will never go out of style, thanks to the efforts of Kelly Browne.

Dorothea Johnson
author, etiquette expert, and founder of
The Protocol School of Washington

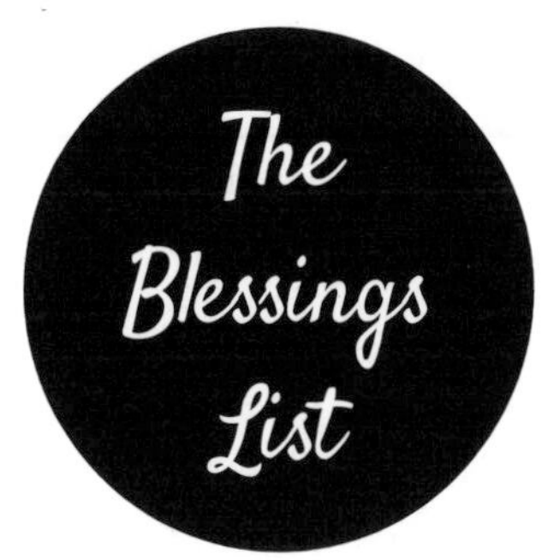

I am grateful for . . .

1. The tenacious and astonishing Linda Konner, whose constant encouragement I am forever grateful for. Thank you for believing in me always.

2. Lynnae Allred and the entire team at Cedar Fort Publishing. Thank you for publishing this book and being missionaries of God's work and global gratitude!

3. Dorothea Johnson—I adore and treasure every single drop of wisdom you have shared with me. Your charm and grace has made an indelible mark on the world and in all of our hearts. We thank you.

4. Charles Kittredge, Norma LeBarron, Jessica Haas and the entire Crane & Co. team in North Adams, Massachusetts. From the desks of kings and queens to currency worldwide, your fine stationery on cotton paper has graced our hands to become treasured keepsakes. Thank you for continuing to be ambassadors of goodwill.

5. Pamela Eyring and the Protocol School of Washington—you are indeed the change we want to see in the world. My gratitude to you and Robert Hickey for your dedication to lighting up global civility is immeasurable.

6. Cindy Haygood, Debra Lassiter, and April McLean of the Etiquette & Leadership Institute—my deepest thanks to you ladies for supporting me and instilling the art of the social graces to give our young adults leadership tools that will last a lifetime.

7. The philanthropic spirit of the women of National Charity League, Inc., San Fernando Valley Chapter, and Terry Anderson, Center Director, Southern California Rose of Tralee—thank you for changing my life and enriching our worldwide community.

8. The academically acclaimed Louisville High School for infusing my education with the keys of the Sisters of St. Louis to heal, unify, and transform the world.

9. All of my extended family, including the Fish, Kerrigan, and Mullens families; the divine Betty Borian; Chris, Aurelie, Stephanie, and Carolyn Mente; my dear friends, especially Robin Prybil, Kim Wileman, Vivian Barone-Finn, the Grabel family, and the Hamermesh family; Steve Blatt; and my wonderful English editor, Lizzie Blatt. My love and thanks!

10. To God and St. Jude—for my wonderful life and the blessings of the people I hold dear to walk beside me, especially my wonderful parents, Richard and Peggy Learman; my brother, Jack Kerrigan; my brother-in-law and sister, Edward Burrier and Gretchen Learman Burrier; my amazing husband, Aric Browne, and our beautiful daughters, Greta and Ava. For you, my heart has no bottom—I love you, endlessly.

Create your Blessing List!
Download a template at www.KellyBrowne.net.

THANK-YOU

(noun)

1. A polite expression of one's gratitude.

Origin of thank-you: from the phrase *thank you* used in expressing gratitude.

First known use: 1792.[1]

Chapter 1

Thank-You Notes 101
The Basics

For as long as we can remember, our parents, relatives, and teachers have never hesitated to remind us to say "please" and "thank you" for just about everything. From saying our prayers for the blessings we have to writing a thank-you note to a grandmother for the gift she sent you, the ever-present prompting of, "Well, what do you say?" seems to never go away, no matter how old you are. There may be moments when you may feel that your mother's constant nagging is driving you crazy, to the point that you refuse to cooperate with her and throw yourself into a tantrum, but she really is trying to help you reap the benefits of being appreciative for what you have in this world to keep those blessings coming back to you. Starting today, take responsibility for choosing the kind of person you want to be, and give the gift of gratitude.

Why Saying "Thank You" Is Important

Besides showing good manners, the reason you thank someone for doing something nice for you or for giving you a gift is you want them to know you are grateful for their kindness. If you don't thank that person, they might feel you didn't appreciate what they did for you and worse, stop remembering you on special occasions! More important, when you thank someone, it makes him or her feel good inside—kind of like the way you felt when you opened your gift.

"Thousands of candles can be lit from a single candle, and the life will not be shortened. Happiness never decreases by being shared."

—attributed to Buddha

Research has shown that sparkly feeling is contagious and gives people a sense of well-being. I call it the magic of gratitude. Get ready to count your blessings and make it your mission to make our world a better place!

The History of Being Thankful

The origin of expressing thanks dates back in time and crosses many cultures and continents. In some form or fashion, the human race has been thanking a higher power for food, water, existence, and continued survival since the dawn of time.

- Ancient Egyptians thanked the Sun god Ra for giving them light, existence, and growth.
- American Sioux Indians thank the earth and sky and ultimately the Great Spirit.
- In Judaism, the Jews thank Yahweh for creation, freedom, and the gift of life in the Hebrew prayer, Modeh Ani.
- In 1621, the Christian Pilgrims gave thanks to God for their survival in America. That day of thanks is celebrated every November on Thanksgiving, a day set aside for thanking God for families and for the food on the table.

With a current world population of over seven billion people and many different religions, it is important to respect everyone's expression of thanks.

How to Write a Thank-You Note in Five Easy Steps

Start feeling good by being grateful for all the blessings in your life and send a thank-you note to brighten someone's day; remember, the magic of gratitude is contagious. Get a piece of nice paper and a good black or blue ink pen, or open a new document on your computer or electronic device:

1. ***Write the Date.***

   January 1, 2015

2. *Write the Salutation, Followed by a Comma.*

Dear (put the person's name here),

Example: Dear Mrs. Browne,

A *salutation* is a greeting or a gesture of welcome like "*Dear*" or "*Dearest.*"

Always use an *honorific* when addressing an adult. An honorific is a word that expresses respect when addressing someone.

Sample Honorifics

Mr. (for all adult men)

Mrs. (for an adult married woman)

Mr. & Mrs. (for a married couple)

Master (for a young man)

Ms. (for a professional woman or if you are uncertain of what honorific to use)

Miss (for an unmarried younger woman)

Coach (for an athletic coach)

Reverend, *Father*, *Monsignor*, or *Rabbi* (for members of a clergy)

3. *Write the Content of Your Thank-You Note.*

Example:

Thank you for the gift card you gave me for my birthday. I am really looking forward to going shopping and picking out a cool drawing book.

- The content of your thank-you note is also known as the *body of the letter*. It is what you want to say or express to the recipient of your note.

- If you don't know what to say, remember it's a note, not a long letter. Just think of the moment when you opened your gift and how you felt when you saw it, and then tell them about it as if they were standing in front of you. Two to three sentences are enough, but be sincere and gracious in what you write.
- Use energetic adjectives and glowing superlatives to help you express your thanks. The "Thank-You Thesaurus" at the end of this chapter is a great reference to help you write your notes.

Example: Thank you for the gorgeous *necklace!*

4. *Write the Closing Followed By a Comma.*

Sincerely,

- The *closing* is the last thing you write before signing your name and informs the reader of your note that your message is ending.

5. *Add Your Signature.*

Ava Meldrum

- Your *signature* is your name, and it is an important part of your note because it tells the recipient who the letter is from—you! Make sure you write your name clearly so it can be easily read.

If you've created your thank-you note on your electronic device or computer and print it out on nice stationery, make sure to sign it with a good black or blue ink pen. All together, your note should look something like this:

SAMPLE CLOSINGS

Sincerely,
Love,
Gratefully,
Respectfully,
Gratefully yours,
Truly yours,
Fondly,
With all my love,
Sincerely yours,
Love always,
Very sincerely,
With affection,
Your friend,
Yours truly,

January 1, 2015

Dear Mrs. Browne,

Thank you for the gift card you gave me for my birthday. I am really looking forward to going shopping and picking out a cool drawing book. I really appreciate your thoughtfulness and hope to see you soon.

Sincerely,

Ava Meldrum

Choosing Stationery for the Perfect Thank-You

> **GRATEFUL SAGE TIP**
>
> **Crane & Co. Stationery**
>
> **Legendary stationery house Crane & Co. has been making gorgeous stationery on cotton paper for over two hundred years. In fact, patriot Paul Revere's banknotes were engraved on Crane & Co. stationery and helped finance the American Revolution. Visit their website at www.crane.com for ideas and to read about their history.**

The kind of *stationery* or writing paper you choose to write your thank-you notes or letters on is important because what you select is a reflection of your personality and should also suit the occasion of your note. Especially in the digital age we live in, your choice of paper, color, size, or weight makes a statement not only about you, but also how you feel about the person you are sending your note to.

- Single and boxed blank cards with a beautiful picture on the front make great thank-you notes. These can be found in museum shops, bookstores, markets, and stationery stores.
- Cards with a preprinted inscription of thanks are also available, but make sure to include your heartfelt note of appreciation written inside. Don't just sign your name! Remember, if someone took the time to do something special for you, it is important for you to thank that person properly.

THE GRATEFUL SAGE

What Is a Monogram?

A monogram is "a symbol that has the first letters of a person's first, middle, and last names and that is put on towels, blankets, clothes, etc., as a decoration or to show ownership."[2] The initial of your last name would appear in the middle, with the initial of your first name on the left and the initial of your middle name to the right.

For example:
Ava Meldrum Browne: ABM

- Make your own thank-you card! Some stationery and craft stores have dozens of paper and envelope selections that can be printed in the store or at home. Don't forget to check out the selection of rubber stamps and inks you can use to design your unique card too.

Social Stationery: The Stationery Wardrobe

As you grow older, the stationery wardrobe is a valuable tool to have on your desk. It consists of different kinds of social stationery and is typically personalized with your name or monogram. Typically, a wardrobe will contain some or all of these options:

Correspondence cards (4¼" × 6½"): This is the most useful stationery for writing short notes, thank-yous, and invitations. Only the front is used to write your note. Some cards include a small design or colored border and are typically a heavier card stock.

Informals (5¼" × 3½"): While their name might sound confusing, informals, or "fold-overs," are formal notes that are folded in half and can be printed with your name or monogram on the front.

Single sheet stationery: Printed with your name and street address at the top, the choice and sizes of these papers are up to you and depend on the length and formality of your letter or note. Lighter in weight, they can fit through a printer, if necessary.

Envelopes: Envelopes are sometimes lined with another color of paper and should include your return address. Including your name is optional.

Calling cards: Calling cards are like personal business cards and are for new friends. They include your personal contact information, such as your name, phone number, and email address. You can simply use your name and phone number or your name and email address—it's up to you. These can be ordered online, in stationery stores, or consider printing your own at home.

The Global Envelope in Four Simple Steps

Now that your thank-you note is written, you need to send it in a matching envelope. Remember, the envelope is just as important as your note because it is the first thing the person you are sending it to sees, so you want to make a good impression. As you would do with any message you write and send to someone else, make sure you check your spelling and write as neatly as you can.

1. The *addressee's first and last name* (the recipient of your note, or to whom you are sending your thank-you note or letter to) should begin at the center of the envelope with the street address directly under it. On the next line, write the city, state, and zip code. The last line is where the name of the country your note is being mailed to should appear.

"Indeed, it is not intellect, but intuition which advances humanity. Intuition tells man his purpose in this life."

—Albert Einstein, Nobel Prize for physics[3]

Here is an example for mailing to an address in the US:

Name of Addressee:	*Mrs. Recipient's Name*
House Number & Street:	*4321 Street Avenue*
Town, State, Zip Code:	*Anytown, ST 80000-4321*
Name of Country:	*USA*

2. Your *return address* (the address of the person sending the thank-you note or letter) should appear in the upper left corner of the envelope or on the back flap. A return address is important because if the post office cannot deliver your note, letter, or package, they will return it to you—the sender. The return address includes your first and last name. Your house number and name of your street should follow on the next line, and then the name of your city, state abbreviation, and zip code, like this:

Your full name:	*Your first and last name*
House Number & Street:	*1234 Street Avenue*
Town, State, Zip Code:	*Anytown, ST 80000-4321*

3. Insert your note, with the front of the note facing toward you, into the envelope and seal it.

4. Place a postage stamp in the correct amount in the upper right corner, and you are ready to mail it!

Your first and last name
1234 Street Avenue
Anytown, ST 80000-4321

Mrs. Recipient's Name
4321 Street Avenue
Anytown, ST 80000-4321
USA

Here are a few examples of how to address an envelope when sending your gratitude to global destinations:

United States of America: www.usps.com

RECIPIENT'S NAME
HOUSE NUMBER + STREET NAME
CITY/TOWN NAME, STATE + POSTAL CODE
USA

Australia: www.auspost.com.au

RECIPIENT'S NAME
HOUSE NUMBER + STREET NAME
SUBURB AND STATE/TERRITORY
POSTCODE
AUSTRALIA

France: www.laposte.fr

RECIPENT'S NAME
HOUSE NUMBER + STREET NAME
POSTAL CODE, TOWN NAME
FRANCE

United Arab Emirates: www.epg.gov.ae

RECIPIENT'S NAME
TITLE and/or COMPANY NAME
PO BOX NUMBER
EMIRATE
UAE

Canada: www.canadapost.ca

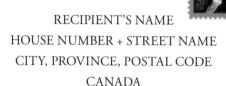

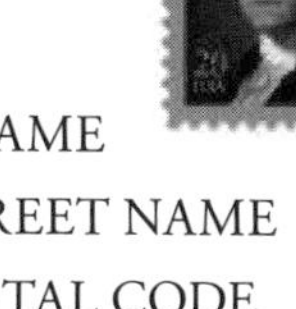

RECIPIENT'S NAME
HOUSE NUMBER + STREET NAME
CITY, PROVINCE, POSTAL CODE
CANADA

Italy: www.posteitaliane.post

RECIPIENT'S NAME
STREET NAME + HOUSE NUMBER
POSTAL CODE, CITY, PROVINCE CODE
ITALY

United Kingdom: www.royalmail.com

RECIPIENT'S NAME
HOUSE NUMBER + STREET NAME
CITY/TOWN NAME, POSTAL CODE
COUNTRY (England/Ireland/Scotland/Wales)
UNITED KINGDOM

Twelve Tips for the Perfect Thank-You Note

1. Handwritten notes on nice stationery are always the best choice when deciding what kind of thank-you note to send.
2. Make your note personal and conversational; write it as if you were speaking with the person who gave you the gift. If you aren't sure what to say, write it out first on a piece of scrap paper or on the computer, and then copy it on nice paper.
3. Never send a note with misspelled words or mistakes. Check your grammar and spelling!
4. Always write neatly using your best handwriting.
5. Remember, the traditional writing instruments to use are black or blue ink, rollerball, or gel pens—never ballpoint pens or pencil. However, expressing your thanks is important, so if you need to use crayons, marker, or colored pencils to show your love—please do.
6. If you are more creative, draw a picture, write "thank you," and sign your name. It's likely that any small gesture of your thankfulness will be appreciated by the person who sent you the gift, so feel free to create something from your heart.
7. Write your thank-you note as soon as you open your gift so you don't forget.
8. Always check to make sure you have the right amount of postage.
9. A thank-you note should be sent within two weeks of receiving a gift.
10. Always call when you receive a gift in the mail so the person who sent it to you knows you got it. You still need to send a thank-you note!
11. If you don't personally thank the person who helped you or gave you a gift, chances are good they won't do it again. So be grateful for your blessings.
12. Even if your thank-you note is late, send it anyway. It will still be appreciated!

The Thank-You Thesaurus: Glowing Superlatives and Energetic Adjectives

Include some of these words to add some pizzazz to your gratitude!

amazing astonishing astounding attractive awe-inspiring AWESOME beautiful beyond belief BRIGHT brilliant COLORFUL dazzling excellent exceptional EXTRAORDINARY fabulous FINE-LOOKING generous gleaming glistening glowing good-looking GORGEOUS HANDSOME hard-to-believe INCANDESCENT inconceivable INCREDIBLE iridescent lively lovely luminous marvelous miraculous MULTICOLORED OUT-OF-THIS-WORLD outstanding radiant remarkable RICH shimmering shining sparkling SPECTACULAR splendid startling striking stunning surprising unbelievable VIBRANT vivid WONDERFUL

GRATEFUL SAGE TIP

If you need help writing in a straight line across the paper, visit my website www.KellyBrowne.net and download the *101 Ways to Say Thank-You* Lined-Paper Template to slip under your thank-you notes.

INTEGRITY

in·teg·ri·ty (noun)

1. The quality of being honest and fair.

First known use: fourteenth century[4]

Chapter 2

Electronic Gratitude

Digital Thank-You Notes & Social Media Success

We live in an exciting time in the world as we witness the explosion of technology. At lightning speed, we are able to universally connect to each other online. As we navigate the electronic frontier, it is important to embrace the amazing benefits we can take advantage of, such as accessing archives from ancient kingdoms in foreign lands, discovering your grandmother's fondness for noodle bowls while video chatting from Beijing, or even watching a live video feed of baby animals in a zoo—we literally have the world at our fingertips. When learning to communicate by the new digital language we are now speaking, it is important to remember our global connectivity and to respect our differences—whether it be race, religion, or traditions—in all we post online. Virtual respect is a key factor in spreading peace, and global gratitude is indeed the silver thread that connects us all.

Remember that regardless of social media website claims of privacy, you are never anonymous, and the pictures you post, comments you tweet, or what you write online will become part of your permanent digital footprint—the trail of all comments and images you post online. Remember your mother's sage advice and "think before you speak." This includes thinking before you write something that cannot be erased, which may affect your reputation or your opportunities for future success. From computers to mobile devices, know that there are many ways to express your electronic appreciation, promote digital respect, and send a thank-you note.

Emails and Proper Formatting for Digital Thank-You Notes

"Believe you can and you're halfway there."

—Theodore Roosevelt, twenty-sixth US president[5]

Traditionally, thank-you notes are always handwritten, but there are certain occasions when sending your electronic gratitude via email is completely appropriate. For example, an electronic thank-you would work when thanking a friend for letting you borrow his or her class notes or when thanking your parent for supporting you. Just remember, in today's digital world, handwritten notes are even more appreciated. They make a personal impact and leave a lasting feeling in someone's heart. The choice is up to you.

Writing an email thank-you note is easy, and its format would apply to any email message you would write and send.

1. *Recipient's Name*

Make sure you have the correct email address for the person you are sending your note to.

2. *Your Name*

It is always a good idea to set your real name in your email preferences so your recipient can quickly identify the email in their inbox. For example, if your email is PFish@internet.com, you would want the recipient's inbox to see your name, properly formatted with correct capitalization, like this: Patricia Fish—PFish@internet.com.

3. *Subject*

To keep your email from heading to the spam folder, provide context in the subject line so your recipient knows what your email is about. For example: "Thank you for the Class Notes!"

4. *Date and Time*

The date and time stamps are automatically included, so there is no need to write them in the body of your note.

5. *The Body of Your Note*

- Salutation—*Dear* or other terms of endearment are always appreciated (but not always necessary for an emailed note). Follow the term you choose with the recipient's name with a comma.
- Recipient's name—Use the recipient's first name or, when appropriate, their title, followed by their sir name. For example, "Dear Margaret" or "Dear Mrs. Kerrigan."
- Your note—Your emailed note should follow the basic spirit of writing a thank-you note as outlined in Chapter 1. Be sure to keep it brief, use proper grammar, check your spelling, review your punctuation, and read it back to make sure it is accurate.
- Emoticons and smiley faces—These little pictures inserted into your message are always fun to use. ☺ Use them for casual messages.

6. *Closing*

When indicating the end of your email, use *sincerely*, *love*, *cheers*, or whatever you feel is suitable for the occasion. Always include your name as your electronic signature. Depending on the situation or recipient, use your first name, full name, or initials.

CAPITAL LETTERS and Exclamation Points!!

Remember, the sound of your voice cannot be heard in an email, and when we text or email, we don't have the benefit of seeing someone's smiling or frowning face, so choose your words carefully to convey your emotion. Avoid using ALL CAPS, or capital letters, when texting or sending an email because it lends itself to be interpreted by the person you sent the email or text to as if you are angry and yelling at them. These are often called "flaming or screaming texts." Likewise, using too many exclamation points also adds heightened emotion to your message. If you are upset, always wait a day before you respond in emotion to someone rather than writing or texting something you will later regret.

Your email should be set up to look like this:

To: Margaret Kerrigan – Margaret.Kerrigan@internet.com

From: Greta Browne – GBrowne@internet.com

Subject: Thank you!

Dear Margaret,

(one space here)

Just want you to know how much I appreciate your sharing the notes for Mrs. Fish's music class with me while I was out of school. Please let me know if you ever need to borrow mine.

(one space here)

Thank you!

(one space here)

Cheers,

Greta Browne

You've Got Mail!—Electronic Mail Tips

1. **Separate your email accounts**. If you have a school-assigned email address, your school will likely have full access to your account. Be smart and only use your school email for communicating with your teachers and classmates. Use your personal email address when communicating with friends and family.
2. **Reply in a timely manner**. If someone has taken the time to email you, reply within twenty-four hours if possible. While some emails don't always require a response, it's a good idea to let that person know you received his or her message.
3. **Forwarding an email**. If you choose to forward an email or send an email that you have received to someone else, make sure you completely read through the entire message you are sending to make sure what you are forwarding isn't going to hurt someone's feelings.

4. **Check your junk mail**. Regularly check your junk mail folder to make sure something important didn't accidently end up in the wrong inbox.
5. **Avoid phishing email scams**. Never respond to any emails requesting money, your personal information, or asking you to enter your password. While some of these emails do look official, show the email to your parents so they can check it by logging in directly to that company's website or by calling on the phone.

Digital Armor: Ten Power Ps to Protect Your Public Profile

1. **Personal profile:** It's always a good idea to protect your name. If you are surfing the web or sending messages, create an online profile name or email address that you can use to keep your real name private and help prevent cyber pirates from stealing your identity. This profile name should *never* include your last name, age, gender, location that you live, or anything that might sound inappropriate or revealing about yourself.
2. **Privacy:** If you are computer savvy, make sure the spam filter, GPS tracking, firewall, pop-up windows, and privacy settings are set on your computer and mobile devices. If you don't know how to do this, ask your parents or the computer lab at your school to help you. These privacy settings are important because they can protect you from unwanted predators and Internet pirates who may try to steal your identity, find your location, or remotely break into your computer without your knowledge.
3. **Place:** Keep your computer in a safe, central place where your parents can help keep you protected, like in the kitchen or family room. Sometimes a parent will notice something that you may not even realize is putting you at risk.
4. **Pirates:** Always block instant messages from strangers online via email or text message. Even if you think you have your settings private, there will always be an inappropriate email, instant message, attachment, or advertisement you are curious to click on. Try to avoid opening these invitations from strangers because

they will capture your information and sell it or try to get more personal information from you.

5. **Pretenders:** Don't ever trust anyone you meet online. Don't tell them where you live or what school you go to. Don't send a picture of yourself or video chat. That person is not your friend. Above all, if someone you don't know is contacting you online and asking you to meet him or her somewhere, insisting you keep it a secret, or threatening you in any way—tell your parents or caregiver immediately. It could save your life.
6. **Protect yourself:** If you accidently visit an "adults only" website, know that these sites track your information and send constant messages to lure you back. Protect yourself and avoid them.
7. **Password protection:** Choose a password that is a combination of letters, numbers, and symbols, and keep it in a safe place at home. Never share your password with anyone other than a parent. If you do, you are allowing the person you gave it to access to your email or the ability to post information online pretending to be you. Be smart and keep the details to yourself—then you won't have to worry about it.
8. **Purchasing:** If you are shopping online, always have the cardholder's permission to use their credit card. It's a good idea to keep one credit card just for Internet purchases if you can, so if the number is stolen, it is easier to track the last place it was used online.
9. **Purge:** Make sure you purge your system regularly by clearing your Internet browser, stored cookies, and any footprints left by companies trying to track your web-browsing history.
10. **Power down:** Make sure you always turn your camera off on your computer when you are finished. If the green light is on, the camera is on, and you want to make sure that no one is looking at you from the other side. Consider taping a little piece of paper over the camera and take it off when you want to use it. Don't forget, Internet hackers can break into your computer without your knowledge, so it's always a good idea to power down your computer at the end of the day to close any possible hacker connections.

Be an Ambassador of Goodwill: Be a Citizen of the World

> *"I've always believed that a lot of the troubles in the world would disappear if we were talking to each other instead of about each other."*
>
> *—Ronald Reagan, fortieth US president*[6]

Our global community knows no bounds. We are human beings and represent many colors of a worldwide rainbow—together we create the light. While we may be separated by borders on land—with different customs, foods, religious beliefs, and languages—together we are the people of the planet earth. For the spirit of the human race to flourish, we must respect and learn from each other. We must remember that every culture has its own traditions and ways of celebrating not only love and family but also life.

The Golden Rules of Texting

- Nothing replaces a great conversation with a good friend in person or on the phone, but sometimes when you're in a hurry, only texting will do.
- Texting is more personal than email because it is immediate and shows up right away on the recipient's mobile device. If what you have to say can wait, then send that person an email.
- When you text, the person you are texting can't see your face or hear your voice, so the spirit of what you are trying to say might be misinterpreted. For example, if you text something that you think is funny to a friend, he or she might not realize you are just joking around and be upset! When in doubt, don't send a text that might be taken the wrong way.
- If you snap a picture and text it to someone else, it's out of your hands forever. If someone sends you an inappropriate or indecent image, be smart and don't text or email it to someone else. Delete it.

- Never text or gossip about anyone, because if that person sees the text you sent, you might end up in trouble over it or it might be sent on.
- Avoid group texts! Sometimes you don't always know everyone you are responding to in the group and might accidently send back an embarrassing message in error!
- Never simultaneously text and drive a car, ride a bicycle, or walk. It's easy to become lost in what you are texting, stop paying attention to what you are doing, and then hurt yourself or someone else. Every text can wait!
- Never text a thank-you! If you want to let someone know how excited you are right away, fine—go ahead and send a text, but follow up with a note of thanks. It will be appreciated!

Smile when you greet someone for the first time, hold the door open for a passerby, give others your full attention when speaking to them, and donate your time to your local school or charitable organization. Strive to be more compassionate and kind to others, especially those with whom you disagree. All are watching—not only our nation's children, but the world.

—Lisa Gaché, Beverly Hills Manners[7]

The Acronym Dictionary: Digital Texting

2MORO	TOMORROW
2NITE	TONIGHT
B4N	BYE FOR NOW
BC	BECAUSE
BFF	BEST FRIENDS FOREVER
BTW	BY THE WAY
BRB	BE RIGHT BACK
CYA	SEE YA
GR8	GREAT
HW	HOMEWORK
IDK	I DON'T KNOW
ILY	I LOVE YOU
IMO	IN MY OPINION
JK	JUST KIDDING
K	OKAY
LOL	LAUGHING OUT LOUD
LTR	LATER
NP	NO PROBLEM
O	HUG
OIC	OH, I SEE
OMG	OH, MY GOSH!
OMW	ON MY WAY
R	ARE
RBTL	READ BETWEEN THE LINES
RL	RUNNING LATE
ROFL	ROLLING ON THE FLOOR LAUGHING
RT	RETWEET
TY	THANK YOU!
THX or THKS	THANKS
TMI	TOO MUCH INFORMATION
TTYL	TALK TO YOU LATER
TYVM	THANK YOU VERY MUCH
U	YOU
WDYT	WHAT DO YOU THINK?
WE	WHATEVER
WYWH	WISH YOU WERE HERE
XOXO	HUGS AND KISSES
X	KISS
Y	WHY?

HONORABLE

hon·or·able (adjective)

1. Deserving honor and respect.
2. Having or showing honesty and good moral character.

First known use: fourteenth century[4]

Chapter 3

Happy Birthday to You!

There is no doubt your birthday and the anticipation of its arrival is exciting! It is the one day of the year where you are honored, celebrated, and solely loved and appreciated by friends and family. From the moment you wake up, the tingling birthday sensation is upon you, and you want the whole world to know it's your birthday. As soon as it's over, you are already dreaming about the party next year. While you might receive gifts wrapped with bright ribbons, remember it's always the gifts money can't buy that will ultimately hold the greatest space in your heart. So embrace the memories of the day, treasure your life and the moments you share with those who adore you, and don't forget to thank all the people who made your special day fabulous or remembered you with a thoughtful gift.

Birthday Netiquette

- Sending a digital thank-you note? Handwritten is always best, but if you want to use your computer or mobile device, check out the "thank-you" apps online. Some stationery apps will allow you to write your note, upload a photo, pull up your contacts, and email, share, or mail as a postcard or note in an envelope for a small fee through the mail.
- Think twice before posting an image of your birthday party on social media websites if you think someone's feelings might be hurt. If you do post, make sure the picture is appropriate and won't embarrass anyone in the photo. There are laws in place to protect people's privacy.
- Avoid thanking someone for a birthday gift on social media sites instead of sending a thank-you note; it's tacky. Social media sites like these are public bulletin boards. If you don't have your

privacy settings turned on, your comments, pictures, and personal information can be read by everyone everywhere.

- Avoid using a text message to thank someone. If you want to let your friend know you got their gift and share your excitement, then go ahead, but you still need to send a formal note of thanks.
- There will be moments in your life when you will not be invited to someone's birthday party. Instead of feeling disappointed or left out, do something special for yourself or someone else, and remember you won't always be invited to everything, nor will you be able to invite everyone to every birthday celebration you have.

"Thanks for Helping Me Celebrate the Day I Was Born!" Sample Notes

Here are some sample notes you can copy, fill-in-the-blank, or use to inspire your gratefulness to help you say thank you to everyone who remembered your special day.

Thank You for Coming to My Party and for the Amazing Gift!

Dear ________________,

Thank you for coming to my birthday party! It was so awesome to have you there to celebrate with me. I really appreciated the [name of the gift] you gave me. It was the one thing I wished for, and I look forward to [playing with it/using it] every day. Thank you for your thoughtfulness.

Love,

____

Dear ________________,

Having you at my birthday was a gift in itself! Thank you for the [name of the gift]. It is perfect, and I love it! I so appreciate your thoughtfulness and generosity.

Your friend,

____

Dear _______________,

You shouldn't have! But I'm glad you did. I loved the [name of the gift]! Thank you so much for your generosity and for helping me celebrate my birthday. See you at school!

Your friend,

____

Dear _______________,

Thank you for coming to my party and celebrating my birthday with me. I can't tell you how much I loved the [name of the gift] you gave me. It's perfect! Thank you for your thoughtfulness.

With love,

____

Dear _______________,

How did you know I wanted a [name of the gift]? I love it! Thank you so much for thinking of me and remembering me on my birthday.

A million thanks,

____

Dear _______________,

Wow! It's perfect. How did you know [name of the gift] was just what I wanted? I really appreciate all the love you put into giving me something so amazing. Thank you for making me feel so special on my birthday and for making my dreams come true.

With love,

____

Dear ______________,

Thank you for making my birthday unforgettable! I love the [name of the gift] you gave me and will treasure it always. The party wouldn't have been the same without you. Thank you again!

Your friend,

____

Dear ______________,

You totally rock! I adore my present—thank you. You really made my birthday a day I will never forget. Thank you a million times!

Love you,

____

Dear ______________,

Wow! What can I say but I adore the fact that you totally gave me the most amazing gift ever. Thank you from the bottom of my heart!

Hugs,

____

Dear ______________,

Oh my gosh! I love it! How do you always find me the perfect gift? I am so grateful for your thoughtfulness and to have you in my life.

With all my appreciation,

____

Thank You for the Arts and Crafts

Dear ______________,

I hope you had as much fun at my party as I did! Thank you again for the [arts/crafts] you gave me. I am already making really amazing [drawings/creatures]. My [mother/father] is so happy I am working on my creativity. A million thanks!

Lots of love,

____

Thank You for the Book or eBook

Dear _______________,

It was wonderful to have you at my party. I just loved the amazing book you gave me. It is such a great story that I can't put it down. Thank you!

Your friend,

____

Thank You for the Clothes or Scarf

Dear _______________,

I cannot wait to wear the beautiful [dress/shirt/pants/scarf] you gave me! How did you know that [color] is my favorite color? Thank you so much for your generosity and for thinking of me on my birthday.

With affection,

____

Thank You for the Computer, Game, Phone, and so on.

Dear _______________,

You always find the coolest presents ever! I couldn't believe it when I opened the box and saw the [name of the item] sitting inside. I kept blinking my eyes thinking that I was dreaming. You do realize that this is the best [computer/game/phone] in the history of my whole entire life? Thank you—you're just awesome!

Love,

____

Thank You for the Gift Card

Dear ________________,

Thank you for the gift card to [name of the store/website]. It's perfect! It was exactly what I wanted, and I can't wait to go shopping. Thank you for the best birthday present ever.

All my love,

____

Thank You for the Stuffed Animals or Doll

Dear ________________,

Thank you for sending my new little friend, [stuffed animal/doll]! You know what? We became friends the moment I opened up your present. [It/She/He] is so soft and cuddly that I just can't stop squeezing [it/her/him]. Thank you for thinking of me and remembering me on my [age] birthday!

Love,

____

Thank You for the Birthday Gift—Digital Thank-You

Dear ________________,

I know I said thank you for the amazing gift, but here's a little snapshot to let you know how much your thoughtfulness meant to me. Sending you a digital hug and squeeze.

Your friend,

____

[INSERT PICTURE OF YOU]

The Global Thank-You Thesaurus

Afrikaans:	Dankie
Armenian:	Shnorhakalut'yun
Chinese (Mandarin):	Xièxiè
Dutch:	Dank je
English:	Thank you
French:	Merci beaucoup
German:	Danke schön
Greek:	efcharistó
Hebrew:	Toda
Hungarian:	Kösz, Köszönöm
Irish (Gaelic):	Go raibh maith agat
Italian:	Grazie
Japanese:	Arigatō
Norwegian:	Takk
Polish:	Dziękuję
Portuguese:	Obrigado
Spanish:	Muchas gracias
Swahili:	Asante
Swedish:	Tack
Welsh:	Diolch

Grateful Birthday Tips

Digital party favors: Have someone take a picture of you with each guest. Here's a great opportunity to send a candid shot along with your digital thank-you note. Consider uploading your party image to a stationery app like www.RedStamp.com to get your thank-you notes done in time.

The History of Birthdays

A *birthday* is the anniversary of the day you were born. World traditions surrounding this once-a-year celebration date back thousands of years.

- Legend has it that the ancient Greeks made round cakes to honor the moon goddess, Artemis, adding a candle to represent moonlight.
- In eighteenth-century Germany, the Germans celebrated kinderfest—birthday celebrations for children that included the use of a lit candle on a special cake. They believed evil spirits visited children on their birthdays and, in an effort to protect the children, celebrated with parties and made happy sounds with noisemakers to scare the evil spirits away.
- By the late 1800s, evidence shows that Swiss birthdays included the use of a lit candle on a birthday cake, representing each year of life to be blown out by the birthday boy or girl.
- Modern Western cultures typically celebrate birthdays with birthday parties, gifts, and the birthday cake with candles; but before the candles are blown out, wishes are made. It is believed that the smoke from the candles carry the silent wishes to the heavens to be fulfilled.

Whatever your family traditions are, a birthday is a moment to celebrate the life you have been given, or the opportunity to stop and honor your loved ones or a friend. Always take the time to be grateful for every single moment you have been given.

The Grateful Sage

If someone gives you a gift or does something that makes you feel uncomfortable, always tell your parents or caregiver so they can help you. In this kind of situation, never worry about hurting someone's feelings or keeping secrets.

Magical Birthday Gemstones

According to scholars, the use of birthstones can be traced back to the Holy Bible's book of Exodus, which describes the Breastplate of Aaron—a religious garment—that was set with twelve gemstones, representing the Twelve Tribes of Israel. Later writings chronicle the belief that wearing these magical stones had healing benefits associated with the astrological signs of the zodiac.

The modern list of birthstones includes:

January	Garnet
February	Amethyst
March	Aquamarine, Bloodstone
April	Diamond
May	Emerald
June	Pearl, Moonstone, Alexandrite
July	Ruby
August	Peridot, Sardonyx
September	Sapphire
October	Opal, Tourmaline
November	Topaz, Citrine
December	Turquoise, Zircon

COMPASSION

com·pas·sion (noun)

1. A feeling of wanting to help someone who is sick, hungry, in trouble, etc.
2. Sympathetic consciousness of others' distress together with a desire to alleviate it.

First known use: fourteenth century[9]

Chapter 4

Spiritual Accomplishments

Coming-of-Age Celebrations

Wherever you are in the world, you have learned your religious customs from your family, and perhaps you've prepared yourself for a coming-of-age celebration in your life. These parties hold great significance because they honor your transformation from the innocence of childhood to the responsibilities of becoming recognized as an adult in your religious community. The following pages list a few worldwide traditions with accompanying thank-you notes.

Bar Mitzvah and Bat Mitzvah

In the Jewish religion, children celebrate their Bar Mitzvah for boys and Bat Mitzvah for girls around the time of their thirteenth birthday. Translated from ancient Aramaic, it means "son (or daughter) of the commandment." Many years of planning go into preparing for this spiritual religious passage into adulthood. From studying the ancient Hebrew holy writings of the Torah to regularly attending temple services and completing a good deed or Mitzvah Project, the spirit of the Bar Mitzvah is to honor God and to reaffirm commitment to Jewish traditions in adult life.

GRATEFUL SAGE TIP

Don't know what to give as a Bar/Bat Mitzvah gift? Consider giving money in multiples of the Jewish lucky number eighteen. For example: \$18.00 × 2 = \$36.00, or \$18.00 × 3 = \$54.00. Why? Because in the Hebrew alphabet, the tenth and eighth letters spell the word chai, which means "life." The popular toast, l'chaim means "to life."

Thank You for my [Bar/Bat] Mitzvah Gift—Money

Dear ________________,

I would like to thank you for joining my family and me in the celebration of my [Bar/Bat] Mitzvah. Having you there to witness this important moment in my life was an honor I will always remember. I truly appreciated your generous gift and will put it toward my future education. Thank you for your generosity and for thinking of me.

With my sincere thanks,

____

Thank You for My [Bar/Bat] Mitzvah Gift

Dear ________________,

Thank you for helping me celebrate my [Bar/Bat] Mitzvah. I love the [name of the gift] you gave me and will treasure it always. Thank you so much for being a part of this special day in my life.

My sincere thanks,

____

Dear ________________,

Just want you to know how much I appreciate your presence at my [Bar/Bat] Mitzvah and celebrating this important moment in my life with me. Thank you so much for the [name of the gift]. It's awesome, and I will treasure it always!

Gratefully yours,

____

Thank You, Rabbi, for Your Spiritual Guidance

Dear Rabbi _______________,

I want you to know how much I appreciate all of your support as I prepared for my [Bar/Bat] Mitzvah—I couldn't have done it without you. Thank you for your patience, for your spiritual guidance, and for believing in me. I did it!

Respectfully yours,

____

Thank You, Mom and Dad, for My [Bar/Bat] Mitzvah

Dear Mom and Dad,

As I write this, I can't believe I have completed my [Bar/Bat] Mitzvah! Thank you for not only supporting me and helping me practice and complete my Mitzvah Project but also for sharing our spiritual traditions so I may pass them on to my children. I will always remember this special day and being surrounded by the love of our family and friends. I hope I made you proud.

Love,

____

Be an Ambassador of Goodwill: The Mitzvah Project

You don't have to be preparing for your Bar/Bat Mitzvah to do a Mitzvah Project. There are many ways you can help someone else in your community, at school, or maybe even in your own family. Here are a few good ideas:

- Volunteer at your favorite charity.
- Tutor someone at school.
- Donate your old sneakers, shoes, or clothes to someone in need.
- Write a letter of thanks to someone who helped you.
- Take a collection of old coats to a homeless shelter.

- Have a bake sale and donate the money to a worthy cause.
- Write a thank-you note to a military serviceman or woman for his or her sacrifice to protect your freedom.
- Help out at home without being asked, make your bed, and keep your room clean.

Perform an act of human kindness for someone else without any expectation of reward. The applause in your heart will make you feel magical.

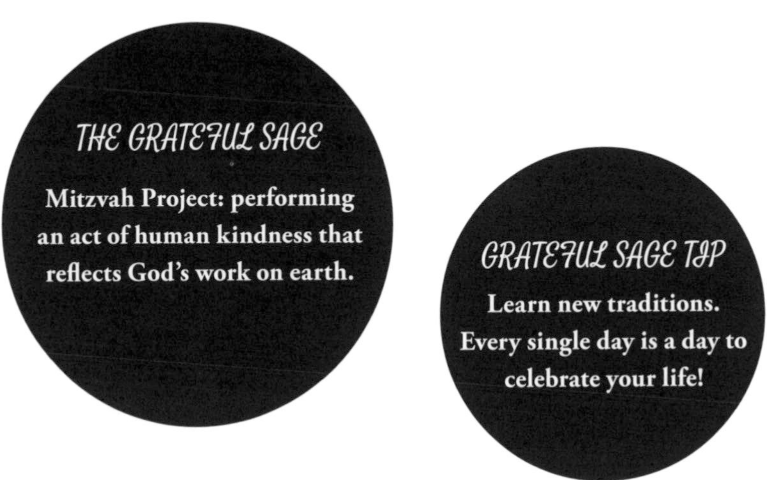

THE GRATEFUL SAGE
Mitzvah Project: performing an act of human kindness that reflects God's work on earth.
GRATEFUL SAGE TIP
Learn new traditions. Every single day is a day to celebrate your life!

First Holy Communion

As Jesus Christ and His Apostles celebrated the Jewish Passover Seder with the sharing of wine and unleavened bread at the Last Supper, so too do Christians in the form of a quarter-size bread wafers and wine through Holy Communion—the most important sacrament of the Catholic Mass. Around the age of seven, Catholic children go through Penance, where they take responsibility for understanding how to be kind, how to love, and how to be sorry and forgiven for all past mistakes. At that point, they are ready to confirm their beliefs in the church. First Holy Communion is a joyous event because it is the first time Catholics are unified with Jesus Christ during the celebration of Mass. Afterward, family and friends gather to celebrate this special occasion, often giving the communicant religious gifts as a way to remember their First Holy Communion.

Thank You for Helping Me Celebrate My First Holy Communion

Dear _______________,

Thank you for celebrating my First Holy Communion with me and for all the love you shared. I so appreciate the [name of the item] you gave me and will keep you in my prayers.

Love,

____

Dear _______________,

Thank you for the blessings you gave me by your presence at my First Holy Communion. I am so grateful for the [name of the gift] and will treasure it always. God bless you.

Love,

____

Confirmation

The Sacrament of Confirmation crosses many Christian faiths. For Roman Catholics, it is the final initiation into the Catholic community, which began with the sacraments of Baptism, Penance, and First Holy Communion. Just like Christ anointed the Apostles with oil on Pentecost, giving them the courage to spread the Christian faith, Confirmation bestows the gift of graces for the soul from the Holy Spirit. When a child is baptized, his or her parents and godparents make promises to raise the child in the light of God's love, to know the teachings of Jesus Christ, and to resist doing harm against others. When a young adult reaches Confirmation, that person takes responsibility for his or her soul's destiny, confirming those promises made in baptism. He or she

"Peace begins with a smile."

—attributed to Mother Teresa, missionary and Nobel Peace Prize recipient[10]

is anointed with the blessed oil of the Holy Spirit. This final Christian rite of passage for these teens is a spiritual journey over a period of two years as they do God's work in their community, attend Mass, are guided by an adult sponsor, choose a new Christian name, and embrace their Christian faith.

Thank You for My Confirmation Gift

Dear ______________,

Thank you for being with me as I received the Sacrament of Confirmation. I really appreciate your prayers of support as I made my spiritual journey and embraced the gifts of the Holy Spirit. I am so grateful for the [name of the gift] and will treasure it always. God bless you.

Love,

____

Thank You for Being My Confirmation Sponsor

Dear ______________,

As I received the Sacrament of Confirmation, I felt so grateful to have you in my life. Thank you for being my sponsor and for your prayers of support for me during this special time. God bless you.

Peace,

____

THE GRATEFUL SAGE

Did you know that part of the Catholic Mass is a symbolic recreation of Jesus Christ's Last Supper with His followers, the Apostles? Jesus and His Apostles were of the Jewish faith and were celebrating the Jews' freedom from slavery on the holiday known as Passover.

Quinceañera

Throughout Latin America, Mexico, and the United States, young girls of Hispanic descent celebrate their rite of passage to womanhood on their fifteenth birthday with a Quinceañera. While traditions vary from country to country, the spirit of honoring this transition is the same and includes the father formally presenting his daughter to society by taking her by the hand and dancing the waltz. This special ceremony is followed by a party, which often includes music, delicious food, and a thank-you speech from the birthday girl. Later in the evening, family and friends will raise their glasses and toast the young lady with the Ceremony of the Fifteen Candles, also known as the Tree of Life—each one representing a special person for the Quinceañera princess and the fifteen years she is symbolically leaving behind in her childhood.

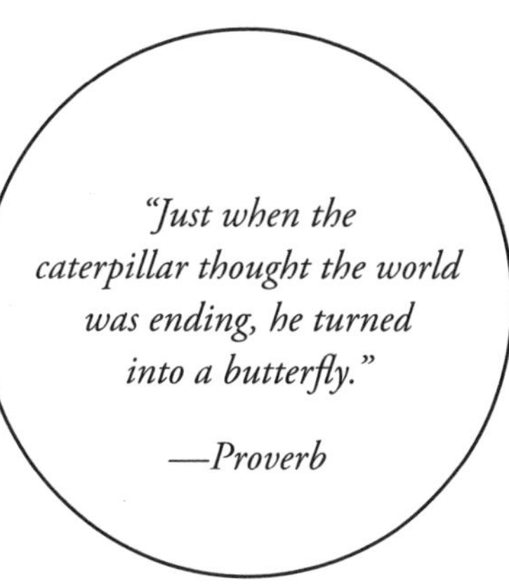

"Just when the caterpillar thought the world was ending, he turned into a butterfly."
—Proverb

In Mexico, the Quinceañera includes the celebration of Mass and the presentation of religious items to the patron saint of Mexico, the Virgin of Guadalupe. Like royalty, the Quinceañera Princess will be accompanied by a Court of Honor, given a sparkling tiara crown and perhaps her first pair of high-heeled shoes, and, in the Mayan tradition, her last doll to symbolize her passage to womanhood. If you are celebrating your fifteenth birthday with a Quinceañera, treasure this wonderful time in your life, count your blessings, and thank everyone who helped make you the woman you've become!

Thank You for Coming to My Quinceañera

Dear ______________,

There is simply nothing more important to me than the love of my family and friends. The celebration of my Quinceañera would not have been the same without you being there! A thousand thanks for the magic of your smiles of support and love for me. I loved the (name of gift), and will think of you every time I (see it/wear it/use it). Thank you!

Love,

____

Thank You, Mami and Papi, for My Quinceañera

Dear Mami and Papi,

Every day I count my blessings to have you both as my parents. From the bottom of my heart, thank you for honoring me at my beautiful Quinceañera but most of all, for guiding me to become the woman I am today. I love you so very much and will remember this day for the rest of my life.

With all my love and appreciation,

____

Thank You to All My Damas, Padrinos, and Madrinas—Quinceañera

Dear ______________,

There are no other words than thank you! Thank you for always being there for me, laughing with me, and picking me up when I needed it the most. As I made my Quinceañera, I could feel your love and support surrounding me. I will cherish the magic of that moment in my heart for a lifetime.

Muchas gracias,

____

Sweet Sixteen Soirees and Debutantes

All over the United States and Canada, girls celebrate their milestone sixteenth birthday with a Sweet Sixteen party. This coming-of-age soiree borrows in tradition from their lovely English counterparts who were presented to society at the legendary Court of St. James in the hopes of finding an eligible suitor of equal social position. Borrowing from the French, English girls from privileged families were known as *débutantes,* or "female beginners," who made their debut or first appearance to society dressed in pure white gowns, elbow-length gloves, and simple jewelry. The debutante, on the arm of her father, is introduced to high society at an elegant ball, kicking off the social season and marking a young lady's transition to a member of society.

Today's Sweet Sixteen soirees vary from extravagant parties to small family gatherings. Like the Quinceañera in Latin countries, Sweet Sixteen traditions may include

The Father-Daughter Dance: Typically a waltz led by her father, the young woman will take the arm of her father for her first dance as he presents his beautiful little girl to the world for the first time.

The Presentation of the Tiara: Acknowledging her daughter's transformation from child to young lady, her mother will crown her with a tiara, celebrating the woman she has become. At this point in a young lady's life, her mother has passed down to her daughter her love, knowledge, and experience—the tools she needs to be a strong woman, ready to take on the world.

The Changing of the Shoes: Borrowed from the Quinceañera, the Sweet Sixteen sweetie will take off her flat shoes and accept the presentation of a pair of high-heeled shoes on a pillow from her father as she walks into womanhood.

The Ceremony of the Sixteen Candles: Each candle on the birthday girl's cake symbolizes and honors the important people who have made a difference in her life. With pride, her parents will light the first candle. The second through fourth candles are traditionally lit by her grandparents, godparents, siblings, or close family members, followed by the seventh through fourteenth candles by her friends. The fifteenth candle is lit by her best friend, and the sixteenth for herself or a boyfriend. Sometimes a seventeenth candle is also lit for good luck!

Down-to-Earth Debutantes

Today's modern debutantes now bow in the Court of Social Consciousness instead of the Court of St. James. While learning the art of the social graces, they also make it a priority to volunteer, raise money, and give back at various charities in their communities. You can make a difference!

Thank You for Helping Me Celebrate My Sweet Sixteen

Dear ______________,

Thank you from the bottom of my heart for celebrating my Sweet Sixteen with me. Having you there filled me with memories I will cherish forever. I really loved the [name of the gift] and so appreciate your generosity. Until we meet again!

Sending you love,

____

Dear ______________,

There are simply no words to express my sincere gratitude for the lovely [name of the gift] and for celebrating my Sweet Sixteen with me. More important, thank you for leaving the gift of your beautiful smile on my heart.

With all my love and appreciation,

____

Thank You, Mom and Dad, for My Sweet Sixteen Soiree

Dear Mom and Dad,

I want you both to know just how much I appreciated the fabulous party you gave me for my Sweet Sixteen! Thank you for celebrating me, supporting me, sacrificing on my behalf, and simply loving me unconditionally. I know I may seem all grown-up, but I will always be your little girl.

All my love, infinitely,

____

A NOTE ON RELIGION AND POLITICS

Take a look around you and notice what is often at the center of much conflict in the world. Most often, fighting takes place when people disagree over power, religion, or politics. Be smart and respect your friends' differences. We could learn so much from each other if we would only listen.

SPORTSMANSHIP

sports·man·ship (noun)

1. Fair play, respect for opponents, and polite behavior by someone who is competing in a sport or other competition.

First known use: 1745[11]

Chapter 5

Team Spirit

Throughout the journey of your life, you will have multiple opportunities to be part of a team and learn valuable life skills that will define the person you will be. At the helm of your team will be your coach or mentor who, ideally, will provide you with the inspiration to achieve your best, challenge your fears, and encourage you to be a leader in all that you do. You may not even realize it, but every day you are part of a team to accomplish certain goals. Whether it's on a sports team, school team, work team, or family team, everyone has an important job to do that is integral to the building of not only your team's success but also yours. Don't forget that crucial to your success are the people who support you, come to your games to cheer you on, and pick you up when you think you can't go on. Be grateful for all these people in your life and, from time to time, let them know how much their love and support has meant to you. A small note of thanks, an email, or a text will fill them with the magic of your gratitude and bring smiles to their faces to know their kindness was appreciated by you.

"The way a team plays as a whole determines its success. You may have the greatest bunch of individual stars in the world, but if they don't play together, the club won't be worth a dime."

—Babe Ruth, baseball legend[12]

THE GRATEFUL SAGE

Inspiration from
Coach John Wooden

Coach John Wooden was a gentleman of grace, inspiration, and dignity who led the University of California at Los Angeles Basketball team to unsurpassed success on and off the court. His now famous Pyramid of Success teaches the valuable keys to achievement in leadership that can be applied to all areas of your life. His philosophy was built on layers that created a foundation for a pyramid, which components he believed lead to competitive greatness as an athlete and a human being.

Pyramid of Success[13]

SUCCESS

COMPETITIVE GREATNESS

POISE, CONFIDENCE

CONDITION, SKILL, TEAM SPIRIT

SELF-CONTROL, ALERTNESS, INITIATIVE, INTENTNESS

INDUSTRIOUSNESS, FRIENDSHIP, LOYALTY, COOPERATION, AND ENTHUSIASM

Team Thank-Yous

Here are some sample notes to send with a card, email, or text:

Thank-You to Your Coach—Any Sport from a Team or Team Player

Dear Coach ______________,

On behalf of [team name], I wanted to thank you for your dedication to our team. You motivated us to strive to work harder, believed in us when we didn't believe in ourselves, and gave us the gift of knowing we could achieve anything with practice, determination, and a little sweat. We want you to know that we will carry with us your inspiring words for a lifetime.

With appreciation and thanks,

____

Thank-You to Your Teammates—General

Hey everyone,

Just wanted to say great game, great focus, and great teamwork out there today! See you all tomorrow!

____

Thank-You to Your Parents for Coming to Your Game—General

Hey Mom and Dad,

I know there may be times when I don't say it, but I really do appreciate you cheering me on at my games and just being there—always.

Love you guys,

____

"Success is peace of mind which is a direct result of self-satisfaction in knowing you made the effort to become the best of which you are capable."

—Coach John Wooden, head coach of UCLA Basketball[14]

Nine Tips to Be a Terrific Team Player

1. **Be Prepared:** Come to practice or school prepared. Eat well, get enough sleep, and keep a checklist of what you need for practice so you don't forget anything.
2. **Be Reliable:** If you have committed to being on a team, be there for practices and games. If you can't, let your coach know in advance so another teammate can fill in for you.
3. **Be a Good Listener:** Listening and paying attention are key to the success of every single team.
4. **Be a Hard Worker:** Nothing in life comes without hard work. You may have talent, but if you want to be good at something, you have to practice to get better or study to get good grades. No one can do it for you. Only you can make it happen.
5. **Be Trustworthy:** There is nothing more important than being a trustworthy person—someone who is honest in what they say and do.
6. **Be Humble:** If someone compliments you for your effort, always be gracious and say thank you.
7. **Be Supportive:** Always show good sportsmanship toward your teammates and opposing teams. Shake hands after a game, and always play fair.
8. **Be Confident:** Believe in what you can do, and don't be afraid to fail. If you do fail, get up again and know that in the process you are one step closer to achieving your goal.
9. **Be Enthusiastic:** Your attitude is crucial not only to your personal success but also to the success of your team. A positive attitude will get you everywhere while inspiring others to follow you.

Team Captain—Be a Warrior

If you've been chosen by your coach to be the team captain, know it's because he or she recognizes your leadership qualities and ability to inspire others to achieve their best when they step on the field, court, or classroom. While the role of captain is an honor, it also carries great responsibility. Your coach will be looking to you to communicate with your team, acknowledge their efforts, and motivate them to victory. Win or lose, what matters most is that each and every one of your teammates knows they pushed themselves to greatness and are proud of the game they played together. Pump up the volume with a few of these motivating texts, emails, and hashtags.

Team Captain—Sample Texts to the Team

ROCK ON, [NAME OF TEAM]!

INSPIRE GREATNESS!

LET'S ROLL, [NAME OF TEAM]!

TOMORROW, WE FIGHT ON!

WAY TO GO, [NAME OF TEAM]! CHAMPIONS!

SAVOR THE MOMENT!

THANK THE FANS!

CAN I GET A, "WHAT? WHAT?"

BOOM! POW! BAM!

BE PREPARED FOR BATTLE!

THANK COACH [NAME]!

THANK THE CHEERLEADERS & SPIRIT SQUAD FOR CHEERING US ON!

Helpful Hashtags

#Inspiring	#Courage	#Grateful
#doyourbest	#Woohoo	#Warrior
#Champions	#TeamWork	#Winning
#TeamName	#101ThankYous	#WorkHard&Win

Team Captain—Sample Emails

[Name of Team]:

Great practice today! Go home, get your homework done, eat well, and get to bed so you can play your best tomorrow. Remember, on or off the [field/court/track], you represent our team and school.

Peace out,

[Captain name]

[Name of Team]:

Remember, as a member of this team, everything you say, do, or write is a reflection on us all. Think before you speak, and be proud of your choices! All for one and one for all!

Cheers,

[Captain name]

Hey [Name of Team]!

Today is *Tell A Teammate Day*! That's right, tell a teammate "You inspire me because. . . ." Get it done!

Fight on!

[Captain name]

[Name of Team]:

Thanks for an amazing season! We tore it up out there, and win or lose, we always played like champions. It's been an honor. Thank you.

[Captain name]

Cheerleaders & Spirit Squad

Part of the thrill of going to competitive games is the excitement of being one with your school as the clock is run out, baskets are thrown, and championship touchdowns are made. Each time you jump up in anticipation of what will happen next, you chime in with the cheerleaders and spirit squad as they pump up the crowd. Beyond their smiles, inspiring chants, and acrobatic flips is a true team of athletes who must work together, be in excellent physical condition in order to perform well, have confidence, and always look their best.

Grateful Sage Tip

Check out the amazing online stationery apps that will allow you to upload a group shot and email your words of inspiration to your team!

As a member of the cheer team, you must be committed to putting your best cheer forward and spreading enthusiasm to everyone in the stadium to rally the team to victory! Remember to thank your cheermates, your parents, and your coaches. Here are a few thank-yous, emails, and text messages to keep the pom-poms twirling.

Thank You for Your Cheerful Team Spirit!

Dear ______________,

Even on the days when I am feeling blue, your cheerful smile always brightens my heart. Thank you for being a ray of light and for all your support on cheer team. You're the best!

Hugs,

____

Dear ______________,

You have a special way of spreading your infectious spirit to all of us. Thank you for being the heartbeat of our team!

____

Hey, ______________!

We were so nervous tonight before the game, and you single-handedly pulled us together to perform at our best. Thank you for motivating the team and bringing everyone together. We rocked it!

____

Seven Cheers for Cheerful Cheerleaders!

1. **Commitment:** Be committed to your team. Be early, practice your routine, and listen to instructions.
2. **Trust:** Be someone whose word is golden. If you say you're going to do something or catch someone, make sure you pay attention and follow through.
3. **Poise:** Be polished, graceful, and elegant in all you say and do.
4. **Attitude:** Be positive and keep a fabulous smile when it's time to raise your pom-poms.
5. **Support:** Be grateful and generous with your support of each other! If someone's kicks are amazing, let them know!
6. **Fitness:** Be healthy, get your rest, eat right, and stretch to help avoid injury!
7. **Confidence:** Be confident. Hold your head up and smile.

Cheer Up Your Community

A great way to bond as a cheerleading team or spirit squad is to spearhead change in your community and represent your school spirit. Your enthusiasm will be infectious and make a difference in someone's life. Consider collecting teddy bears for your local children's hospital or outgrown winter coats for the homeless, or take part in an Act of Kindness Day. Whatever you do, your spirit will be appreciated!

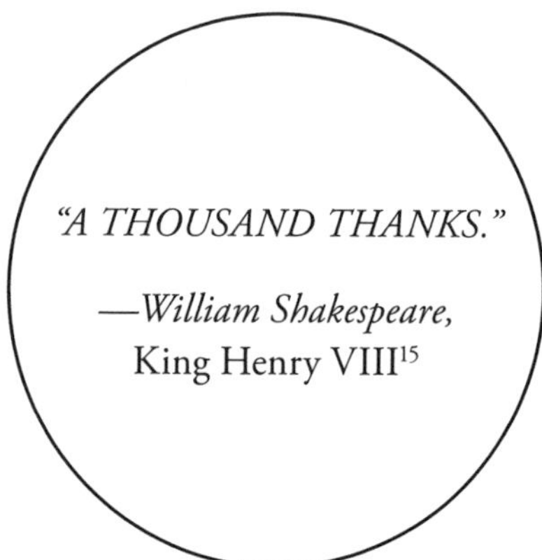

"A THOUSAND THANKS."
—*William Shakespeare,*
King Henry VIII[15]

Quips from Grateful US Gold-Medal Olympians

"If you don't have confidence, you'll always find a way not to win."

—Carl Lewis, track & field[16]

"In the end, it's extra effort that separates a winner from second place. But winning takes a lot more than that, too. It starts with complete command of the fundamentals. Then it takes desire, determination, discipline, and self-sacrifice. And finally, it takes a great deal of love, fairness and respect for your fellow man. Put all these together, and even if you don't win, how can you lose?"

—Jesse Owens, track & field[17]

"Sports knows no sex, age, race or religion. Sports gives us all the ability to test ourselves mentally, physically and emotionally in a way no other aspect of life can. For many of us who struggle with 'fitting in' or our identity—sports gives us our first face of confidence. That first bit of confidence can be a gateway to many other great things!'"

—Dan O'Brien, decathlete[18]

"Focus, discipline, hard work, goal setting and, of course, the thrill of finally achieving your goals. These are all lessons in life."

—attributed to Kristi Yamaguchi, figure skating

"The things you learn from sports—setting goals, being part of a team, confidence—that's invaluable. It's not about trophies and ribbons. It's about being on time for practice, accepting challenges and being fearful of the elements."

—Summer Sanders, swimming[19]

CIVILITY

ci·vil·i·ty (noun)

1. Polite, reasonable, and respectful behavior.

First known use: 1533[20]

Chapter 6

Thank You for Being My Friend

The gifts we treasure most in life don't always arrive in a huge box tied with blue satin ribbons. They are the unseen gifts of love and support from our friends that we sometimes assume will always be there. While we can't always see or hold these small acts of kindness in our hands, they are cherished in our hearts forever. In your journey through life, know that some friends may come into your life for a short period of time, while others may stay a lifetime. Whatever amount of time a friend walks the road of life with you, the spirit of that friend will leave footprints in your heart. Through life's balance of time, celebrations, and disappointments, a true friend will always be there. So the next time you receive a little help from your friends, let them know you appreciate them!

The Top Twelve Tips to Be a Grateful Friend

1. **Happiness**—It's never someone else's responsibility to make you happy. It's all yours. Remember, thoughts are things; what you think you are, you will become. Choose to be happy and make good life choices that you are proud of and empower you.
2. **Friendship**—To have a friend, you must be a friend. Remember to never treat anyone in a way that you wouldn't treat yourself. If someone is behaving disrespectfully toward you, it's up to you to set a boundary with that person or walk away from him or her. No one has the right to be mean to anyone—ever. Be a role model for people to follow.
3. **Listen**—Sometimes when friends just want to talk, you just need to listen.
4. **Frenemies**—Don't ever be jealous of others or of their successes. For example, if they get good grades, it's because they study. It's up to you to work hard in your life to make your dreams come true.

THE GRATEFUL SAGE

The Admiration List

An amazing way to brighten a friend's or classmate's day is to create an Admiration List and let that person know what qualities you admire most about him or her. Communicating even the small things you like can have a significant impact by showing that person the effect he or she has on us. For example, letting your friend know you love his or her laugh because it makes you laugh, or letting a shy classmate know you think he or she is an amazing artist or writer can change that person's life. Create your own list or visit www.KellyBrowne.net and download The Admiration List, or ask your teacher to start one in your class.

5. **Respect**—Tolerance and respect for your friends' political and religious beliefs if they are different from your own is really important. You might learn a new way of looking at life you never considered before.
6. **Compliments**—Always tell your friends you admire them and offer your heartfelt congratulations when they do well.
7. **Cliques**—You are known by the company you keep, so take a minute and look at the quality of friends you surround yourself with. Whether you realize it or not, you will end up copying their habits, good and bad. Surround yourself with people who have qualities you admire and who inspire you to bring out your best.
8. **Gossip**—If someone gossips to you, he or she gossips about you. It's always the people that have the inside scoop on everything that you need to be cautious of.
9. **Pay Attention**—Notice how a person treats others. Chances are good he or she will end up treating you the same.

10. **Breathe**—If people hurt your feelings, never do something to deliberately cause them harm. You will regret it. The best revenge in life is to be successful! Besides, always remember that you decide how someone makes you feel.
11. **Forgiveness**—If someone has offered a sincere apology, move on and learn from the experience. If you can't forgive and forget, don't hold on to the resentment toward that person. Your negative feelings will cause you more harm than good. Let it go.
12. **Get Help!**—Sometimes you or a friend will have problems you can't solve by yourself. Don't be afraid to ask a parent, teacher, or even your doctor for advice.

Thank You for Being a Friend Notes

Here are some thank-you notes to thank the friends who have made a difference in your life and helped make your world a better place.

Thanks for Making My World a Better Place

Dear ________________,

I want you to know how much I appreciate having you in my life. You make my world a better place—thank you!

Hugs,

____

Thanks for Supporting Me

Dear ________________,

I really appreciate all the help and support you have given me. From the bottom of my heart, I'm sending you a squeeze.

Your friend,

____

Thanks for Supporting Me—Inspiring You Too!

Dear ________________,

Be the leader I know you are. Have faith in your dreams and become the legend you're destined to be.

Rock on,

____

Dear ________________,

Have faith in your heart to follow your dreams. I believe in you!

Hugs,

____

Dear ________________,

Life is filled with challenges. It's how we stand up to them that will define the person we will become. Rise up and be the warrior you are—you're ready.

Peace,

____

Thank You, Just Because

Dear ________________,

You know what is so amazing about you? I don't even have to say a word, and you understand what I mean. Appreciate all that is you!

Love,

____

Dear ________________,

Thank you for accepting me exactly how I am and never trying to change me. Please know I treasure our friendship.

Love you,

____

Thanks for Being My Bestie

Bestie,

You're so awesome! Best day ever. Thank you for your love, support, and friendship!

Your Bestie,

Me

Thanks for Everything, Here for You Too!

Dear ________________,

I know if I ever needed anything at all, you would be there. Near or far, I'm here for you, too—always.

In my thankful heart,

____

Dear ________________,

I don't know what happened, but if you need me, I am totally here for you to talk or simply to hold your hand. Thinking of you.

Hugs,

____

Thanks for Understanding—I Am Sorry

Dear ______________,

I am sorry I hurt your feelings and I hope we can be friends again.

Your friend,

____

Dear ______________,

The separation between us has made me feel blue. If there was anyone in my life I enjoyed hanging out with, know it was you.

Miss you,

____

The Grateful Sage

The Power of Social Media

Social media has changed the world in ways no one could have ever imagined. With the intended spirit to be a force for good and shared technology, social media has also helped topple corrupt governments in distant lands and given the people of the world a voice when they felt they could not speak. Use it to spread peace.

Digital Citizenship Dos & Don'ts

- **Do** think before you speak, and think before you write something you will regret online. Even if you delete your post or picture, someone can take a screenshot from anywhere in the world of what you wrote, so think before you post!
- **Do** remember that when you write something, it doesn't always come across in the same spirit as if you said it in person. So make sure nothing you write can be misinterpreted. If you write something in CAPS, it can be perceived that you are sending a screaming text.
- **Do** remember that even though you may have privacy settings turned on, nothing on the Internet is private because your friends may show what you've posted or texted to someone else. There is also the chance that their parents are checking their mobile devices and computers too.
- **Do** tell your parents or caregiver when you receive a threatening message from someone who's bullying you. Take a screenshot and email it to your parents or yourself before it's deleted. Consider taking steps to protect yourself, like reporting the incident to the police department, your school, or your internet service provider, and make sure to block that person from being able to contact you.
- **Do** immediately remove an online post or picture of someone if he or she asks you to delete it. You'd want the same done for you.
- **Do** avoid getting yourself caught up on anonymous social websites. It's a waste of your time and energy when you could be doing something more productive and beneficial toward achieving your dreams—nothing is anonymous.
- **Do** remember that when you send out a group text, not everyone may realize that everyone in the group can see other people's responses.
- **Do** be careful when you send out a group email or receive one. Know that there is a difference between responding directly to the person who sent the email with *reply* and *reply all*, which is a reply to everyone.

- **Don't** ever give out your friends' contact information, passwords, or personal information to anyone. Let them do it themselves.
- **Don't** ever email, text, or post on social media a photo of someone that might be harmful to his or her reputation—you will get in trouble and end up regretting it.
- **Don't** ever use bad language online. It makes you look foolish and vulgar, and that's the way people will think of you. If friends use bad language on your page, delete it. If they complain about it, tell them, "Hey, it's not cool." If they continue it, you can use your privacy settings to control or block who can post to your page.
- **Don't** ever send, say, or post threatening messages to anyone—ever! Even if you are just kidding, because the tone of your voice can't be heard. You can be expelled from school, or your action might cause that person to retaliate against you. So if something happens, cool off first. Talk to your parents or school before you make a mistake you will regret.
- **Don't** overshare your personal information online. Posting a picture winning an award at school of the spirited cheerleading team or a snapshot of your family on vacation is wonderful, but you never want to write all about your personal life drama. Keep it private! You will be happier you did.
- **Don't** tell anyone the password to your email address, phone, school webpage, social media account, or online shopping site. While you may feel that you can trust someone with absolutely anything in one moment, anyone can make a bad decision and do something regrettable. If you have given out your password, change it immediately to protect yourself and your reputation.

Famous Thank-You Notes

Dear George,

Remember no man is a failure who has friends. Thanks for the wings!

—Clarence, *It's a Wonderful Life*[21]

Dear Toad,

I am glad that you are my best friend.

Your best friend,

—Frog, *Frog and Toad Are Friends*[22]

Grateful Sages through the Ages

"If you want to know what a man's like, take a good look at how he treats his inferiors, not his equals."

—J. K. Rowling, author of *Harry Potter and the Goblet of Fire*[23]

"No matter what happens in life, be good to people. Being good to people is a wonderful legacy to leave behind."

—Taylor Swift, recording artist[24]

"Associate yourself with men of good quality if you esteem your own reputation; for 'tis better to be alone than in bad company."

—attributed to George Washington, first US president[25]

"No person is your friend . . . who demands your silence, or denies your right to grow."

—Alice Walker, author

"The antidote for fifty enemies is one friend."

—attributed to Aristotle, Greek philosopher

"For beautiful eyes, look for the good in others; For beautiful lips, speak words of kindness; And for poise, walk with the knowledge that you are never alone."

—attributed to Audrey Hepburn, actress and humanitarian

DIGNITY

dig·ni·ty (noun)

1. A way of appearing or behaving that suggests seriousness and self-control.
2. The quality of being worthy of honor or respect.

First known use: thirteenth century[26]

Chapter 7

Count Your Blessings

Celebrating Love and Life

In this tech-savvy world we live in, it's easy to become swept up in dazzling gadgets, the pressures of school, and relationships while forgetting the blessings that are most important in our lives. Thanks to the Internet, it feels like we can purchase anything we want online, and with a click, it will arrive on our doorstep the next day. Remember the Egyptians who filled their pyramids with grand chambers of jewels and gold to take with them into the next life? All those beautiful material possessions were left behind, filling museums for all of us to study and enjoy.

You see, the riches in life are around you right at this moment—they are the things that money can't buy. My mother always says, "The items we have in this life are just ours to borrow." It is really true. Remember that your life is the gift, and embrace the real treasures in this world in the lives of the people you hold dear to your heart, not how much stuff you have. Pay attention to the little things along the way, and communicate your appreciation to the people who work hard to provide for you. Visit your grandparents or thank your mother for taking care of you or your father for working late to make sure you have the opportunities he might not have had. Later, you will realize all these little magical moments in your life are the big things you remember most. Tell the people you love that you love them so you don't look back and wish you had. Find a reason to celebrate your life every single day.

There are many ways to express your thanks to the people in your life who love and support you. Here are a few creative ideas you can do to make a difference.

Five Ways to Keep Your Blessings Coming

1. Tell the people you love that you love them!
2. Say thank you. When you say thank you, it makes people feel good inside that you acknowledge the thoughtful act they did for you or for the item they gave you. Remember, the magic of gratitude is contagious. If you don't thank people, chances are good they will stop helping you or giving you things because they will think you are ungrateful.
3. Say please if you want something. It makes a difference and is a sign of respect. If you don't say please, your request for something feels like a demand, and it might cause the person you want something from to not give you what you want at all.
4. Listen and pay attention to the people who are there to support you. Always look in someone's eyes when they speak so they know you are listening.
5. Do nice things for others without being asked. Clean up the dishes after a meal, fold the laundry, pick up your towel, ask your brother or sister if they need help with their homework, or call your grandmother and wish her a happy birthday. Simply being kind will have its rewards.

"Thanks for Being a Blessing in My Life" Notes

Sometimes the best messages we receive are the ones we don't expect. It's the notes that stop our day for a moment and swell our hearts because someone took the time to write something special just because they were thinking of you. In the same way that your family and friends lift you up and tell you what a great job you did, they too need those

"We are taught you must blame your father, your sisters, your brothers, the school, the teachers—but never blame yourself. It's never your fault. But it's always your fault, because if you wanted to change you're the one who has got to change."

—Katharine Hepburn, Academy Award winner, Best Actress[27]

same affirmations. The next time you want to brighten a family member's day, don't wait for Mother's Day. Send a text, email, or card to your loved ones or leave them a little note of appreciation.

GRATEFUL SAGE TIP

Use the Grateful Hero's Thesaurus in Chapter 9 to help you describe how amazing your mother or father is to you!

Thanks, Mom, for Your Love and Support

Mom,

I am so lucky to have you as my mom. I love you!

Love,

Me (XOXOXO)

Mom,

I know sometimes it doesn't seem like I appreciate everything you do for me, but I do. Thanks, Mom. I love you.

Love,

____

Mom,

You are the most beautiful woman in the world. Thank you for always taking care of me, loving me, listening to me, and somehow understanding everything. I really love you, Mom.

Your favorite child,

____

Thanks, [Dad/Grandfather], for your Love and Support

Dear [Dad/Grandfather],

I love you because you are [adjective], [adjective], and [adjective]. Thanks for being someone I can always count on!

Love,

____

Dad,

I hope one day I am as wise and wonderful as you are to me. Thanks for supporting me and being there when I need you. Love you, Dad.

Love,

Me

Thanks for Being My Sister

Dear ______________,

Even though you are [older than I am/younger than I am] and we argue sometimes, I do love you all the time. I am always here if you need someone to talk to.

Love,

____

Thanks for Being My Brother

Dear ______________,

Thank you for helping me. I am so lucky to have a brother like you.

Love,

____

Thanks, Grandmother, for Everything

Dear Grandma,

I know I don't see you every day, but I want you to know that I think of you and all the nice things you do for me. I love you so much.

Love,

____

Thanks, Grandma and Grandpa, for the Visit

Dear Grandma and Grandpa,

Thank you for coming to visit me this weekend and helping to take care of me. I love seeing you both and hearing all the funny stories you tell about my [mother/father]. I hope I see you soon.

Love,

____

Dear Grandma and Grandpa,

I had so much fun at your house [this weekend/yesterday/this summer]. Grandma, I loved every delicious [cookie/cake/meal] and so appreciated the love you put into everything you do. Grandpa, thank you for all the advice you give me. I am so lucky to have grandparents like you. Love you to the moon and back.

Love,

____

Fundraising for Schools, Teams, and Clubs

There may come a time when you need to reach out to your family and friends and ask them to buy raffle tickets, candy, cookies, or something fabulous to help you raise money for a cause. When you ask for everyone to support you, always make sure to sincerely thank them for their donation. If you don't, they might not be so quick to help you in the future. If you are raising funds online, most sites will allow you to thank everyone by email, but if you need to go the handwritten route, here are some quick thank-you notes you can use.

Thanks for Your Donation to My School, Team, or Club

Dear Friends and Family,

I am so grateful to all of you for helping me raise money to support my [school/club/team]. Thanks to your generosity, we will be able to [briefly say how donations will be used: buy new uniforms, fund art supplies, build a new library, and so on]. It is because of your support that we will be able to accomplish our dreams. Thank you for helping me!

Love,

____

"'Tis a far, far better thing doing stuff for other people."

—Amy Heckerling, screenwriter, Clueless[28]

Thanks for Buying Raffle Tickets for My School Fundraiser

Dear _______________,

I just want to let you know how much I appreciate your buying raffle tickets for my school. I am really grateful for your support and hope you win!

Love,

____

Notable Notes from Inspiring People

Remember these inspiring words because, in life, the choices *you* make determine who you will be and the person you become your whole life long.

"Your time is limited, so don't waste it living someone else's life. Don't be trapped by dogma—which is living with the results of other people's thinking. Don't let the noise of others' opinions drown out your own inner voice. And most important, have the courage to follow your heart and intuition. They somehow already know what you truly want to become. Everything else is secondary."

—Steve Jobs, visionary and cofounder of Apple[30]

"We can't help everyone, but everyone can help someone."

—attributed to Ronald Reagan, fortieth US president

THE GRATEFUL SAGE

Notes on Jealousy

Jealousy is "an unhappy or angry feeling of wanting to have what someone else has."[29] The reality is, jealously is the absence of being grateful for what you have and being envious that someone has more things than you do. Never envy others for how smart they are or if they have more money than you do. Remember, if people gets good grades in school, it's because they study. If they have money, it's because they worked to get it. It's common sense. If someone makes you feel jealous, look inside and let it inspire you to change your life. Don't make excuses or call someone names. Focus on your own journey and what you need to do with your life—no one can do it for you. It's up to you.

"The greatest glory in living lies not in never falling but in rising every time we fall."

—Nelson Mandela, former South African president and Nobel Peace Prize winner[31]

"What I've learned is not to change who you are, because eventually you're going to run out of new things to become."

—attributed to Taylor Swift, recording artist

"We are what we repeatedly do. Excellence then is not an act, but a habit."

—Will Durant, author, paraphrasing Aristotle, Greek philosopher[32]

"I speak to everyone in the same way, whether he is the garbage man or the president of the university."

—Albert Einstein, Nobel Prize for physics[33]

THE GRATEFUL SAGE

The Blessings List

There is nothing more powerful than counting your blessings and being grateful for what you have in this world. Make a list of what you are grateful for, or visit www.KellyBrowne.net and download the Blessings List. Any time you are feeling blue, take out this list and write one more thing you feel appreciative of. Recording everything—including the food on your table, your parents, friends, health, or the roof over your head—can change your life.

101 Ways to Say Thank You: The Blessings List

I am grateful for these blessings in my life . . .

RESPECT

re·spect (noun)

1. A feeling or understanding that someone or something is important, serious, etc., and should be treated in an appropriate way.

First known use: fourteenth century[34]

Chapter 8

Love and Thanks

Blessings of Love and Friendship

There is simply nothing more amazing in life than that sparkly feeling of love when you look into someone's eyes. Your heart races, you can't sleep, and you find yourself doodling instead of paying attention in class, wondering where that person is under the riot of stars in the sky. Call it puppy love, true love, or destiny, the next time you think he or she is the one, remember there is a whole wide world of amazing people you will meet throughout your life, so take your time. Embrace every single magical moment you have with the people you love and keep these tips in mind when you say, "I heart you!"

Love—Love is a strong and constant feeling of affection for someone and is felt in different ways and at varying times throughout our lives. Know that you will love many people in your life, and in many different ways—maybe for a moment or perhaps a lifetime. Whatever amount of time you have together, cherish it.

Crushes—Having a crush on someone or really liking someone is sweet. Know that your life will be filled with many people you think are fabulous!

Soul mates—It is believed that when destiny finds your soul mate or the person who is your perfect match, you will know by the sparks of magic you share. A true soul mate will love, honor, and support your life decisions through the good times and the bad.

Love yourself—Always love yourself first and make choices that are right for you. No one can love you unless you love, honor, and respect yourself first. Be classy and act like a lady or gentleman. Don't ever dumb yourself down.

Be yourself—Don't try to change yourself to be something you aren't just to make someone like you—it won't work out in the end. Be authentic!

Honesty—Don't ever be afraid of sharing your truth. If you like someone, tell them when the time right, and if someone expresses love for you, it is always better to be honest, in a kind way, if you don't feel the same way. Above all, never start being untruthful to someone because you are afraid he or she will be upset with you. If you cannot be honest with the person you love, or if that person is dishonest with you, rethink your relationship with him or her.

Everything comes to those who wait—Your time is precious. If someone doesn't share your feelings of love, remember you can't force him or her to love you back, no matter what. If your crush likes someone else, don't try to hang on to them. Let that person go with all the love you had. While your heart may be a little broken in the moment, rest assured there are many fish in the sea, and in time, another will come swimming along.

Pay attention—Always pay attention to how someone behaves, because how he or she treats others is how he or she will eventually treat you. No one has the right to treat you badly, hurt you, lie to you, or treat you with disrespect, no matter who they are.

Don't judge a book by its cover—Remember, the quiet or shy kids are sometimes the kindest, so take the time to know someone's heart. Choose someone who is gorgeous inside and out!

Respect yourself—If someone you love is asking you to do something you feel isn't right, don't do it. Always respect yourself in all you say and do. If that person walks away because you refuse to do what was asked—good riddance!

Third-wheel friends—Rather than sending messages to a friend or loved one through a mutual friend, deliver the message yourself. Involving a third person in any drama between you and someone else will ultimately result in miscommunication. If you are asked to be the messenger, stay out of it!

Jealously—If a friend you love begins to show signs of jealousy, really pay attention to that. Jealously is a sign of someone's personal insecurity, and you will never be able to change him or her. While it may seem momentarily sweet that a friend is jealous because you are giving your attention to someone else, that kind of behavior is not okay. It is controlling and can intensify over time to the point that you might be afraid to speak to or hang out with other people because you're worried about upsetting that person. Find someone else with more confidence in themselves.

> *"All you can take with you is that which you've given away."*
>
> —*George Bailey's office wall,* It's a Wonderful Life[35]

Love in a Digital World—Social Media Tips

Communication—Don't let texting replace conversation. It's not the same. The sound of someone's voice is a gift not to be missed. In all relationships you have in life, it is important to listen to what someone is saying and to look that person in the eyes when he or she speaks—even if you don't agree or have anything to say.

Cyberstalking—Social media was designed to allow people to share and exchange information about what's going on in our lives. Make sure you pay attention to how many times you are cyberstalking others' pages simply to see where they are, who they are with, or what they are doing. Instead, pay attention to what's going on in your life.

Oversharing online—Be careful of oversharing your personal problems on social media websites. Remember, everything you post is public, and everyone can read it for a long time to come. Definitely avoid posting cryptic messages in order to call someone out publicly—it makes you look bad.

Posting selfies and personal integrity—Selfies with your friends sharing your achievements, cute pictures of your leopard kitty, or a gorgeous day at the beach are posts we love to see on social media. Remember, all the images you post are part of your permanent digital footprint, so make sure they are fabulous and don't compromise your integrity in any way that could affect your future.

Facetime, video chat, and Skype—Remember when you video chat that everything you say and do can be captured by the person you are virtually talking to in a screenshot and posted without your permission.

The Grateful Sage

Lord Learman and the Power of No

I treasure the wisdom of my father, Richard Learman. He is a man of tremendous talent who, inspired by Shakespeare, listens to many but speaks to few and is lovingly regarded as Lord Learman in the Entertainment Industry. With his elegant demeanor, stage presence and commanding voice, his sage advice has always been, "Learn to say no if you don't want to do something. When people question you why, simply say, 'because I choose not to,' reminding us to stand firm on the choices you make in your life. Don't ever do something you don't want to do in the hopes someone will like you. One single moment can change your life forever." If you make a mistake, take a look at yourself to see how you can learn from the choice you made and move forward.

"What a man does for others, not what they do for him, gives him immortality."

—attributed to Daniel Webster, American orator and statesman

The History of Valentine's Day

For hundreds of years, people all over the world have celebrated St. Valentine—now considered the patron saint of love—on his feast day, February 14. Mystery surrounds the legend of Valentine, but he is remembered as a third-century Roman priest whose quiet acts of kindness to spread love were known only to God. Today's modern traditions surrounding this heartfelt day include the following:

- *Images of the angelic winged baby, Eros, known to the Greeks as the god of love and later renamed by the Romans as Cupid, holding his bow and arrow.* The legend goes that if Cupid hit you with his arrow, you were destined to be love-struck. A heart with Cupid's sharp arrow sticking through it is still a widely used symbol of love. For centuries, poets and painters alike have used the image of Cupid to depict tales of romance and passion.
- *Bouquets of roses, given to loved ones as tokens of affection.* The color of the roses carries an additional message to the recipient:

Red = Love   **Orange** = Gratitude

Pink = Affection   **Yellow** = Friendship

White = Weddings and new beginnings

- *The color red.* Red is the color most associated with Valentine's Day because it is the color of the heart.
- *Candy and chocolates.* These are given as sweet gestures of appreciation for a friend, classmate, or sweetheart. From heart-shaped red velvet boxes to pastel-colored sugar conversation candies with cute inscriptions of love, the possibilities to spread love are endless!
- *Valentine's cards, notes, and letters.* These are probably the most popular and cherished of all the global traditions. Whether they are purchased in a store or made at home, these Valentine messages on paper are an opportunity to express your personal affection to your family, classmates, friends, and sweethearts and are treasured keepsakes for a lifetime.

Celebrating Valentine's Day Every Day: Little Love Notes of Appreciation

Celebrating love is wonderful any time of the year. Use some of these notes to let your sweetheart know you adore him or her.

Dear _______________,

Will you be my valentine?

Love,

Me

Dear _______________,

I love you with all my heart. Until we meet again . . .

Love,

____

Dear _______________,

You are the light of my life and the magic of my soul.

Love you!

____

Dear _______________,

Every time I close my eyes, I see your face.

Love,

____

Dear _______________,

Your laughter is my favorite song.

I heart you,

____

Dear _______________,

When you look at the moon, know I am looking at it too and thinking of you.

Miss you.

With all my love, always,

____

Dear _______________,

In my hands, I give you my heart.

Love,

____

Dear _______________,

In your hands, know you hold my heart.

____

Dear _______________,

No matter where you go, know my love is with you always.

Love,

Me

Dear _______________,

You are my everything.

Love you,

____

Dear ______________,

You are my sunshine.

Love,

____

A Note on Trusting Your Intuition

We are blessed to live during a time when the benefit of technology has given modern mankind many comforts our ancestors did not have. Most of us can walk into our kitchen, open up the refrigerator, grab the milk and cookies, and eat them—never once stopping to think about how lucky we are to have shelter and fresh food.

In ancient times people had to rely on all of their senses to simply survive, and without the gifts of vision, hearing, smelling, tasting and touch, they could have died. Even more important, they needed to rely on the combination of these senses with their *intuition*, or that little voice inside your head that tells you something isn't right about someone or a situation. Intuition is your immediate sense of knowing something. It's the uncomfortable feeling you get inside you when you just simply know someone isn't being truthful with you—you can't explain it. You just simply *know.* If you are sensing something isn't right about someone's behavior around you, pay attention, and tell your parents or someone you trust. Your intuition is like an internal warning system to help you sense danger. Trust it—it could save your life.

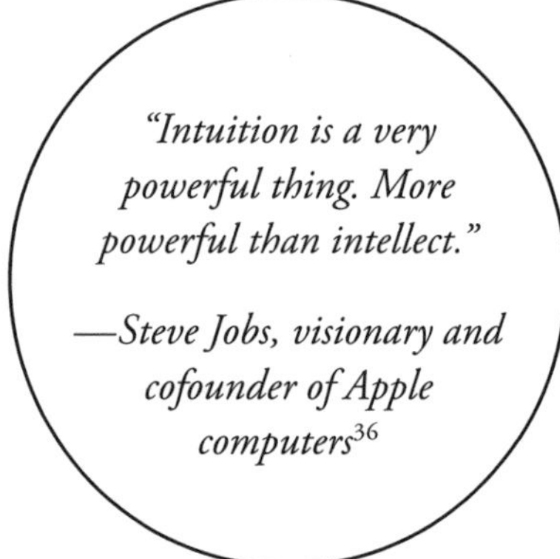

"Intuition is a very powerful thing. More powerful than intellect."

—Steve Jobs, visionary and cofounder of Apple computers[36]

Valentine's Day: Shakespearean Phrases of Love

"I would not wish any companion in the world but you."

—*The Tempest*[37]

"Good night, good night! Parting is such sweet sorrow, that I shall say good night till it be morrow."

—*Romeo and Juliet*[38]

"Love looks not with the eyes, but with the mind, and therefore is winged Cupid painted blind."

—*A Midsummer Night's Dream*[39]

"Hear my soul speak. Of the very instant that I saw you, Did my heart fly at your service?"

—*The Tempest*[40]

"Doubt that the stars are fire, Doubt that the sun doth move, Doubt truth to be a liar, but never doubt I love."

—*Hamlet*[41]

"A heart to love, and in that heart, Courage, to make's love known."

—*Macbeth*[42]

DETERMINATION

de·ter·mi·na·tion (noun)

1. A quality that makes you continue trying to do or achieve something that is difficult.

First known use: fourteenth century[43]

Chapter 9

Knowledge Is Power

Electric Keys to the Future: Education & Empowerment

For thousands of years, grateful sages have long emphasized the simple fact that knowledge is power. It's true, being grateful for what you have—along with your education—are the keys to your success. The ability to read is essential, and the more you know about the world and its history, cultures and people, the more you will benefit from that information.

With technology at our fingertips, you have the ability to access observatories all over the globe and view our stellar universe in ways the ancients could only dream of. You can read about the past mistakes of others to figure out how to do something better because a great idea can come from anywhere. Were it not for the tenacity of inventors like Benjamin Franklin and Thomas Edison, we may not have the benefits of electricity we rely on today, but because of the knowledge these men shared with us and because of the teachers who inspired them, these ideas grew from small thoughts to illuminate the earth. Their ideas became dreams, and through the power of what they had learned they turned those possibilities into realities that changed and advanced mankind forever.

So the next time you are dreading going to school, facing an exam, or wondering if you should go to college and extend your education—think again. The more you know, the more you will be more successful in your choices. Education will lead to better life decisions.

"Education is the most powerful weapon which you can use to change the world."

—Nelson Mandela, former South African president and Nobel Peace Prize winner[44]

The Grateful Girl's and Guy's Six Gems of Knowledge

It's important to remember that there are many ways to learn. Whether it be in the traditional forum of the classroom, in home-schooling, through the lessons of life, or from our elders and mentors, opportunities to learn new things are around us every day. Keep these grateful tips in mind as you collect your gems of knowledge on the path to success.

Being grateful can increase your grade point average. It's true. Research has shown that maintaining a positive attitude and appreciating what you have can keep you happier, maintain your focus in school, and help you achieve better grades.

Respect your elders. At this moment, you might feel as if you know more about life, school, and what goes on in today's world than your parents or grandparents. On some level you may be right, but remember that the adults around you have had many of the same life experiences you have had but perhaps in a different way. Don't be afraid to ask for advice and to appreciate the great wealth of life experiences they can share with you.

Work for it. Instead of complaining about all the things you don't have, be grateful for all the blessings you do have. If you really want something that costs more than you have, take the steps to earn the money you need to buy it or save up your allowance. When you realize what it takes to earn money, you will quickly see how hard you need to work to earn that dollar. Let it inspire you!

Get your college degree. Going to college is essential to your success because your educational degree will give you the foundation of information you need to move forward in the career you want to be in. Whatever your dreams are, there are many ways to get the financial assistance you need to go to college. Check in with your college counselors to research all your options and ask about scholarships you might be eligible for. From online classes to community colleges, there is always a way to accomplish what you set out to do.

Pay attention. Listen when people speak. If you can't hear in the classroom, ask to be moved closer to the front of the room to help you stay focused. Even if you think you know everything there is to know, throughout your life you never stop learning, and there might be one new thing you learn that changes everything.

Deal kindly with difficult people. You will encounter many difficult people, but it's how you choose to handle them that will make all the difference. Difficult people are often miserable, ungrateful people who take out their anger in the form of bullying someone else, and that behavior is unacceptable. They may come in the shape of classmates, teachers, employers, acquaintances, or even family friends. Always choose to step away from these kinds of people and let your parents and school administration know what's going on. Remember, you have a long life, and difficult people are only in your life for a temporary amount of time—never let them get the best of you.

"Give a man a fish and you feed him for a day.

Teach a man to fish and you feed him for a lifetime."

—Chinese proverb

The Inspiration of Teachers, Mentors, and Senseis

Becoming a teacher is a great honor, life achievement, and responsibility. A teacher can be anyone who instructs others on how to do something so they can learn to do it for themselves and then pass that knowledge on to others so they can learn. Almost everything you do must be learned, and there must be someone to teach you.

From learning to tie your shoes to learning to drive a car, someone must take the time to share what he or she has learned with you. Teachers are there to provide us with the information we need to keep moving forward. Take a moment to honor those people around you who have made a difference and influenced your life as you reach for the stars.

"Thank You, Teacher, for Your Inspiration" Notes

Dear Mrs. ________________,

I want you to know how much I have enjoyed being in your class this year. I have learned many wonderful things I did not know about the world. Thank you for all of your words of wisdom and inspiration.

With appreciation,

____

Dear Mr. ________________,

Thank you for believing in me and supporting me along the way. I will never forget the lessons I learned in your class. Thanks for everything.

Sincerely,

____

Dear Ms. ________________,

Thank you for opening my eyes to new possibilities around me. Your enthusiasm made your class so much fun for us to be in that we actually looked forward to [name of subject] every day. Thank you for making a difference in our lives.

All the best to you,

____

Thank You, Mentor, for Your Words of Wisdom

Dear [Mrs./Ms./Mr.] ________________,

It has been an honor and a privilege for me to work and learn from you over the [last few months/last year]. Thank you for not only inspiring me to achieve great things in my life but also for being a mentor I can look up too.

With my gratitude,

____

Thank You, Sensei

Dear Sensei ________________,

When I walked into the dojo, I thought I knew everything. Thank you for patiently teaching me the art of self-control, determination, strength, and power within. I am grateful for the wisdom you shared.

Respectfully,

____

Thank-You to a Guest Speaker

Dear Mrs. ______________,

On behalf of the [name of the group/school/class], I wanted to express my thanks to you for attending our [name of month] meeting and for speaking on [name of subject]. Please know we appreciated not only the time you took to speak to us but also the wonderful information you shared, and we look forward to applying it in our lives. Thank you so much!

Sincerely yours,

____

"The successful warrior is the average man, with laser-like focus."

—attributed to Bruce Lee, martial artist

Inspiration from the Master of Myths—Joseph Campbell

The masterwork of Joseph Campbell and his piece *The Hero with a Thousand Faces* uncovered the blueprint of archetypes and heroes in the great stories, myths, and legends from around the world. His work was fascinating and became a guide for authors and storytellers everywhere, inspiring modern story consultant Chris Vogler to create a guide for motion picture studio executives that became the best-selling book *The Writer's Journey.* You will recognize the path of The Hero's Journey across many motion pictures and television shows as an ordinary person who stands up amidst challenges to make a difference in the world and who is transformed by their experiences to become a hero. Visit www.thewritersjourney.com for more information.

"A hero ventures forth from the world of common day into a region of supernatural wonder: fabulous forces are there encountered, and a decisive victory is won: the hero comes back from this mysterious adventure with the power to bestow boons on his or her fellow man."

—Joseph Campbell, *The Hero With a Thousand Faces*[45]

The Hero's Thesaurus

Use these heroic adjectives to describe someone in your life and to inspire the hero you will become.

beautiful brave charismatic charming CLEVER courageous courteous DETERMINED friendly FUNNY GENEROUS gracious handsome honest honorable KIND magical PENSIVE selfless smart strong SWEET thoughtful TRUSTWORTHY valiant

THE GRATEFUL SAGE

Be a Hero and Master of Your Domain

Stop for a moment and visualize your life as if you were looking down at a map from above. Now look where it is you want to go. What is it that you want to achieve? If you look at your map closely, you will see that there are many roads that will lead to the same destination. On those often-prickly paths, it is the ordinary woman or man who must walk those roads and encounter all kinds of barricades in the shape of tricksters, false friends, or challenging experiences. Those difficult moments are really opportunities in disguise to help you appreciate all the treasured things you have and help to shape your character to propel you forward and define the hero you will become. The gems of wisdom we receive from our parents, teachers, and mentors along the way are gifts to enhance our journey. Some people will walk that path with us for only a short period of time and then turn at the fork in the road to take another path to their own destinations, while others may walk with us for a lifetime. On that road, remember to embrace your mistakes because they help you learn to do something right the next time. What's important is to get up when you fall, no matter how many times you have to. Always keep trying and move toward your dream to become the hero you are destined to be.

Climbing the Ladder of Success: School & Job Interviews

School interviews are just the first of dozens of interview opportunities you will have as you venture out into the world. The purpose of an interview is for you and the interviewer to get to know each other, and it provides a unique opportunity on a personal level to present yourself and to ask and answer questions about school or career possibilities. Always follow up with a thank-you note within twenty-four hours of your interview to thank your interviewer for his or her time. Whether it is emailed or handwritten and mailed, that note of appreciation will make you stand out over the other applicants. While it isn't necessary to include your résumé, use this note to include your contact information, media links, or for any additional ideas you might have that you forgot to mention in the interview. How well you write this note will reflect how you present yourself and what kind of representative you will make for the school or company. More important, you are demonstrating that you are not only smart but also a person with excellent values and social graces. Keep these things in mind when sending your note of gratitude.

- Keep your note short, concise, and limited to one page. Be sincere and professional in what you write. Know your audience, and maintain the appropriate level of formality in your salutation and closing.
- Proofread your letter. Always read it out loud and use the spell-check tool in your text program or email. Check for correct punctuation and proper grammar. You can miss an opportunity simply because you were sloppy.
- Always use black or blue ink for handwritten notes, and follow the format guidelines outlined in Chapter 1.
- Always follow up with a thank-you note within twenty-four hours of your interview.
- Mention again your desire for the position or place at the school. Clarify any uncertainties the interviewer might have expressed, and show your strengths.
- If you are mailing the note, always use a matching envelope. Be sure to check the address you are sending it to and include your return address.

- Ask your interviewer for his or her business card so you have all the correct information to refer to. If you have ordered or created your own calling card or business card, include it with your note as an easy reference to contact you.
- Think of creative ideas to help your thank-you note stand out. Look at the school or company colors, mascots, slogans, or the location of the school as sources of inspiration.

Computer-Generated Thank-You Note—The Basics

Typically used following interviews or for professional notes of appreciation, the computer-generated thank-you note allows you to write your thank-you note on your text editing program. In fact, many of these programs offer letter templates you can choose from, with customizable letterhead to meet every situation. After you have written and spell-checked it, print it out on beautiful stationery, sign it in blue or black ink, and mail it.

The Format of a Computer-Generated Thank-You Note

The format of a basic computer-generated thank-you note includes proper spacing, the date, and company contact information, as well as your personal contact information.

It should look something like this:

April 26, 2016

(date at the top of the page, and four line spaces between the date and name)

Mr. Richard Learman
Learman University
450 Center Drive Lane
Palo Alto, CA 94301

(two line spaces between the last address line and your salutation)

Dear Mr. Learman: *(use a colon here instead of a comma)*

(one line space here)

It was a pleasure to meet you today and I appreciate your taking the time to allow me to speak to you in person and answer all my questions. I really enjoyed learning about the groundbreaking opportunities in the (area of interest) Department at Learman University and believe the exciting program offerings will challenge me toward a successful career in (field of study). As we discussed, please find the link to my (online portfolio/website/résumé) below.

(one line space between paragraphs)

Thank you again for considering me as a candidate for next year's Learman University freshman class. If you have any further questions, please don't hesitate to contact me. I look forward to hearing from you soon.

(one line space)

Sincerely,

(four line spaces—handwrite your name)

Kelly Browne
youremailaddress@internetmail.com
mobile number
website address link for your online portfolio
social media links

Thank You for the College or University Interview

Dear Ms. ________________,

I wanted to follow up on my interview with you this afternoon and let you know how much I appreciated your taking the time to meet with me. I enjoyed getting to know you and learning more about [name of school]. While I know you are considering thousands of applications, allow me to assure you that attending [name of school] has been a lifelong dream of mine that I have worked for throughout my academic career. I am confident that my well-rounded background and history of volunteer service will help me be a better student at your school and an asset to your community. I would not trade those life experiences for anything. Thank you for considering me as a candidate for next year's Freshman class. If you give me the opportunity, I know I will make [name of school] proud.

Sincerely,

____

Thank You to the College Guidance Counselor

Dear Mr. ________________,

Thanks for all your help and support. I have made the decision to attend [name of college] in the fall. I am so grateful to you for your guidance and encouragement through the entire process. Thank you for everything and for believing I could do it!

With my appreciation,

____

Thank You for the Letter of Recommendation

Dear Ms. ________________,

Words can't express my gratitude for the beautiful letter of recommendation you wrote for me [for my college applications/to add to my résumé]. Please know how much I appreciated the time you took to write it. A million thanks for your kindness.

Sincerely,

____

Global Interview Tips from the Etiquette & Leadership Institute

Southern girls know a thing or two about being perfectly polished! Keep these tips in mind from Cindy Haygood, Debra Lassiter, and April McLean of the Etiquette & Leadership Institute when you head out to your next interview.

Appearance: Make sure when you go to your interview that you are dressed appropriately, wearing clean clothes and polished shoes. Always be properly groomed, freshly shaved, and showered.

Résumé: Always bring a copy of your current résumé that includes your accomplishments.

Timing: Arrive on time! Being late sends a message to your interviewer that you don't value the time he or she is taking to meet with you. Make sure you look up where you are going ahead of time and be early.

Research: Research the company or the school and the classes or degree you are interested in so you can ask intelligent questions. Don't be afraid to write down those questions and bring them with you.

Manners: Mind your manners! Sit up straight, say please and thank you, and remember you are not born with good manners; you must learn them.

Impression: Eye contact and a good handshake are key. Stand up when you leave your interview and shake your interviewer's hand, thanking them for taking the time to meet with you. For more information, please visit www.etiquetteleadership.com

Kick It up a Notch: Volunteering, Internships, and Part-Time Jobs

It's never too early to start thinking about your future life plans. Keep these tips in mind as you venture forth on your road to college and career and light up the universe.

Volunteering for Success—A great way to help you get job experience on your résumé is to volunteer at a charitable organization. Not only will your community benefit from your acts of kindness, but you will also feel good about your contributions and help others, not to mention your service will look impressive on your future college and job applications. Make sure when you volunteer to ask the organization you are working with to give you a letter of recommendation that includes the number of service hours you gave, your qualities, and what your job responsibilities included so you can give it to a future employer along with your résumé.

"Why fit in when you were born to stand out?"

—attributed to Dr. Seuss, author

Part-Time Jobs—Depending where you live in the world, opportunities for part-time jobs are everywhere. Everything including babysitting, tutoring, working at a summer camp, and filing papers in an office for a family friend give you an opportunity to earn extra money. Here too, always ask for a letter of recommendation that you can use to help support your future endeavors. These letters are little votes of confidence in you from past employers that set you apart and give you credibility that you are someone to believe in.

Internships—Similar to a part-time job, internships are opportunities for on-the-job training and experience, though they are often unpaid. An internship will afford you the ability to work in a company that gives you direct contact with the people who could ultimately hire you and realize how your hard work and creative ideas will benefit them. Internships also give you the unique opportunity to work in the environment or the career you are interested in to see if it is, in fact, something you want to pursue. You can find internships in high-tech companies, motion-picture studios, government agencies, and even law or doctor's offices around the world. If there is a company you'd like to work for that doesn't have an internship program, ask if they'd create an opportunity for you. Many colleges and universities also have college credit internship programs and work with students to help propel them toward their future endeavors. Some students are hired after graduation by the companies they interned for. As always, get a letter of recommendation at the end of your internship to help you secure a future job position.

"If you can dream it, you can do it."

—Tom Fitzgerald, Disney Imagineer[46]

Using Digital Tools for Your Success

The worldwide web allows us to access information on anyone, anywhere, and at any time. Keep these virtual tips in mind to pave the way to your success.

Your Online Reputation—Colleges, universities, future employers, and business associates will often run an Internet search on you to research your online behavior. The pictures you post and comments you make will most likely be viewed, discussed, and considered before you are accepted or hired. If you are concerned about anything you have posted, delete it if you can.

Create an Online Résumé—If you are working a part-time job, internship, or have community service credits, at some point you will want to lay the foundation to create an online résumé as a quick reference for future opportunities. Check out places like www.LinkedIn.com and take a look at the résumés of people you admire in your field of study or at the companies you would like to work at. You will be amazed at how different everyone's personal journey to success is. Let it inspire you and be a trailblazer.

Create a Paper Résumé—Having a résumé is an absolutely necessary tool to your success because people want to see your educational level, contributions to your community, accomplishments, awards, athletic history, and other personal details. If you don't know how to make one, look for ideas online, ask your school counselor or parent to help give you guidelines, and look at the text editing program on your computer for a template you can fill in. You might also include a small professional picture of yourself on your résumé so your interviewer will remember you.

Digital Thank-You Notes—Handwritten notes are always best, but in this world of instant communication, sometimes the emailed thank-you note is the most efficient and effective. Refer to the section on emails and proper formatting of digital thank-you notes in Chapter 2 for tips on how to send your electronic gratitude for your interviews. Thank-you notes allow you the opportunity to follow up with your interviewer and set you apart from the competition.

Creating a Blog or Website—The explosion of technology has given everyone everywhere a voice and the unique opportunity to showcase personal talents. If you have something important to say, advice you want to share, ideas for better ways to do something, a portfolio of your creative genius, filmmaking talents you want to showcase, or a story you want to tell—you can. With your parent's permission, you can set up your own blog, website, or channel to create your destiny. Be sure to include the link to your site when you follow up with your interviewer so your information can be quickly accessed.

Take a Note from *Modern Manners* . . .

Actress Liv Tyler has learned a thing or two from her grandmother Dorothea Johnson, etiquette expert, author, and founder of the Protocol School of Washington. In their best-selling book, *Modern Manners*, she writes:

> Receiving a handwritten card or thank-you note is always exciting. Even something as simple as an email or text shows your appreciation if you don't have time to write a note. When I meet with a director to discuss a future project, for example, I follow up with a note letting him or her know how much I enjoyed our meeting and express my passion for the project. This is a very nice way to let someone know you're sincere, and it leaves a memorable impression and sets you apart from others.[47]
>
> —Liv Tyler

"Thanks for the Opportunity" Notes

Use some of these notes to send to people who took the time to help you out.

Thank You for Meeting with Me for the Summer Job

Dear Mrs. ________________,

Thank you for meeting with me today and considering me for the [name of the job] position at [name of the camp/company/office]. I know working on your team would be an amazing opportunity for me this summer and that I would do an outstanding job. Again, many thanks for your consideration, and I look forward to hearing from you soon. If you have any questions, please don't hesitate to contact me.

Sincerely,

____

Thank You for Considering Me for the Internship

Dear Ms. ______________,

It was a pleasure to meet with you today. I want to reiterate that working at [name of the company] would be an amazing opportunity and that I am willing to work hard to learn everything I need to know. I assure you, I am someone you can count on who will be loyal and reliable. Thank you for considering me for this internship.

Most sincerely,

____

Thank You for the Opportunity—Letter of Recommendation Request

Dear Mr. ______________,

As you know, my time working at [name of company/charitable organization] is quickly coming to an end. I would so appreciate it if you would write me a letter of recommendation that I can use toward my future endeavors. Thank you for the opportunity you have provided me with and for the wealth of experience you have given me.

Sincerely,

____

And the Envelope Please—Celebrity Thank-You Speeches and Shout-Outs

Being able to hold the award-winning statuette in your shaking hands takes a lot of hard work, sacrifice, and dedication. The celebrities know when the winners are announced, they must stride up to the microphone and thank the list of people in their lives who have helped them along the way. Pay attention to the thank-you speeches from celebrities who are grateful for the support they have received from their fans, family, and friends to help them achieve their dreams. You might even try writing your own acceptance speech!

PEACE

(noun)

1. A state in which there is no war or fighting.
2. An agreement to end a war.
3. A period of time when there is no war or fighting.

First known use: twelfth century[48]

Chapter 10

Winter Holidays

As the leaves change their colors from shades of green to hues of red and gold, it's a clear sign that the winter holidays are quickly approaching. The weather feels chillier, and depending upon where you live, flurries of icy crystal snowflakes may fill the air. No matter what your spiritual beliefs, the joys of the holiday season are exciting as we are swept up in a winter wonderland of brightly colored lights, striped candy canes, glittering Christmas trees, and spicy gingerbread men as we await the arrival of that jolly elf, dear old St. Nick. It's a joyful time of giving to each other, shopping for presents, celebrating miracles, and commemorating events that changed mankind.

Embrace these moments when you are surrounded by family and friends, for it is here that memories are made around a table, laughter is heard as stories are shared, traditions are continued, and loved ones are dearly remembered. These are, indeed, the greatest gifts in life to celebrate. Never forget, the season of gift giving is more than your Christmas wish list. It's about being grateful for what you have, appreciating what you receive, and giving to someone else from your heart. Bring your joy to the world and spread holiday cheer.

Worldwide Winter Spiritual Celebrations: Hanukkah, Kwanzaa, and Christmas

Learning about the international customs that are celebrated in your own community is exciting because it gives you more opportunities to discover ideas, embrace new traditions, taste exceptional foods, and celebrate! If your spiritual beliefs are different from a friend's, respect that friend by taking a moment to learn about his or her holiday celebrations or share a special treat with your classmates that might be part of your tradition. No matter what your belief systems are, there is always a common thread in the importance of living a life of gratitude. Here's a snapshot of how our friends around the globe enjoy the holidays:

The Miracle of Hanukkah: The Jewish Festival of Lights

Hanukkah, also known as Chanukah, is the Jewish holiday celebrating the rededication of the second temple of Jerusalem in 164 BC. It also commemorates the story of the single-day supply of oil that burned miraculously in the temple for a period of eight days. Meaning "dedication" in Yiddish, the season of Hanukkah begins on the twenty-fifth of Kislev on the ancient Jewish calendar and includes the ceremonial lighting of a candle each night on the menorah lamp to remember the miracle. This spiritual holiday is filled with traditional foods and the exchange of gifts—traditionally chocolate and gelt coins, which means "money" in Yiddish. Many children will play with a four-sided spinning top called a dreidel. The dreidel is marked with a Hebrew letter on each side that together stand for *Gadol Hayah Sham,* or "a great miracle happened there."

Kwanzaa: An African Celebration of Family, Community, and Culture

Created in 1966 by African-American author and scholar, Dr. Maulana Karenga, Kwanzaa—meaning "first fruits" in Swahili—is a spiritual seven-day holiday season from December 26 through January 1. Embracing the traditions of the African harvest celebrations, it is a deeply meaningful time of remembrance in the global African community, as each day is dedicated to one of the Seven Principles: Unity, Self-Determination, Collective Work and Responsibility, Cooperative Economics, Purpose, Creativity, and Faith. Gifts of books are typically given to children to remind them of their rich ancient history, along with the symbols of Kwanzaa reflecting the African culture. For more information, please visit www.officialkwanzaawebsite.org.

Christmas: Celebrating the Birth of Jesus Christ

On Christmas Day, December 25, Christians everywhere celebrate the birth of the Savior or Messiah. Believed to be the Son of God, Jesus Christ's spiritual teachings of love would become the belief system we know today as Christianity. Christ was born in a manger over two thousand years ago, and news of His birth was carried by heavenly angels to shepherds tending their flocks, who traveled to see the child. Later, three kings known as the Magi followed a brilliant light, the Star of Bethlehem, across the sky bringing gifts of gold, frankincense, and myrrh, kneeling in honor before Him. The legacy of Jesus Christ became history. For more information, visit your local library or do an Internet search to read how Christ's work continues in the world today.

Merry Christmas Traditions

Christmas: The word *Christmas* comes from an Old English phrase *Christ's Mass*. Roman Catholics celebrated the birth of Christ on His chosen feast day of December 25 by attending Mass in His honor, which became known as Christmas.

Gift Giving: The gifts the Magi brought Christ are remembered in the exchange of presents on Christmas. Gift giving is also symbolic of the importance of giving to others. Giving someone a Christmas gift does not have to cost a lot of money. Think about creating a piece of art, baking holiday cookies, or simply sitting down and writing your own holiday story for someone else. What matters most is that you remember the important people in your life during this time and letting them know

THE GRATEFUL SAGE

Live Holiday Greetings

Most grateful guys and girls know how to connect friends and family around the world by accessing their digital tools. Not everyone can be together on holidays, so remind the party to video chat on their computers or mobile devices. This way, you can have dinner together, open gifts, and connect virtually. Create your memories.

they are special to you. Because it's on the calendar on the same day every year, you have plenty of time to plan ahead.

Christmas Trees: Winter festivals date back to the ancient custom of decorating evergreen trees with fruit as a symbol of eternal life in winter, when nothing grows. By the mid 1800s, the popularity of the Christmas tree had grown worldwide and become a universal symbol for the holiday. Those who celebrated often placed a star at the top to remember the star of Bethlehem. Today's Christmas trees are adorned with sparkling lights, ribbons, bells, ornaments, candy canes, and religious symbols.

Christmas Cards: John Horsley created the first Christmas card in London in 1843, with illustrations of celebrating families performing acts of kindness and giving to the poor. Sending holiday cards with inscriptions of "Merry Christmas" became wildly popular and continues today. If you want to remember everyone in your life but can't buy everyone a gift, sending them a Christmas card during the holiday season is always a wonderful surprise to receive in the mail, or even by email—which won't cost you anything.

The North Pole and Santa Claus: It would simply not be Christmas without Santa Claus and his workshop of magical toy-making elves at the North Pole! Every grateful girl and guy knows the importance of staying off the Naughty List in the hopes that on Christmas Eve, St. Nick will fly his sleigh, stuffed with toys for every girl and boy throughout the world. Flown by his team of reindeer across the starlit sky, Santa lands on rooftops and magically descends down chimneys to leave presents under Christmas trees while carefully stuffing stockings with treats. No matter how old you are, remember it's important to thank even Santa for all the lovely holiday gifts he brings. On Christmas Eve, leave him a letter beside the tree, thanking him for coming and wishing him well until next year. He's sure to appreciate a few Christmas cookies and a glass of milk too.

"Thank You for the Holiday Gift" Notes

As soon as you've torn off the brightly colored ribbons and bows, you're bound to hear one of your parents say, "Oh, you've got to send a thank-you note to your grandmother for that!" If you don't, you can count on the fact that your grandmother is at least expecting you to call and thank her. Here are a few holiday thank-you notes to help you keep the holiday gifts coming for years!

Thank You for the Holiday Gift—Digital Thank-You

Dear ________________,

Words could not express my excitement when I opened your [name of the holiday] gift! Thank you for bringing joy to my world! I love it! Merry everything! [INSERT A PICTURE OF YOU HOLDING UP THE GIFT]

Thank you,

____

Thank You for the Holiday Gift

Dear ________________,

How did you know exactly what I wanted for [name of the holiday]? I have been wanting the [name of the gift] so much you don't even know! I really appreciate your thoughtfulness and I thank you for giving it to me. Wishing you a [Merry Christmas/Happy Hanukkah/Happy Holiday] and a Happy New Year!

Love,

____

Dear ________________,

Thank you so much for thinking of me! I loved the [name of the holiday] gift you [gave me/sent me] and am looking forward to [playing with it/using it/wearing it]. It means so much to me that you thought of me, and I thank you for your kindness. I hope you had a wonderful holiday and wish you a Happy New Year!

Love,

____

Thank You for the Holiday Gift—To a Classmate

Dear ______________,

It was really sweet of you to give me a [name of the holiday] gift, and I really appreciate your thoughtfulness. I hope you have a wonderful vacation and get everything you wish for! See you in the new year!

Your friend,

____

Thank You for the Holiday Gift—Book

Dear ______________,

I am excited to start reading [name of the book]! Thank you so much for getting it for me. I have had it on my wish list and have wanted it desperately. Thank you for giving me a little holiday cheer and a reason to curl up by the fire. Happy Holidays!

Love,

____

The Grateful Sage

Think about buying holiday cards at after-Christmas sales, when they are often half the price. Use them to send your holiday thank-you notes or save to send a greeting next year.

Thank You for the Holiday Gift—Clothing

Dear ________________,

I love it! Thank you very much for the [cool, gorgeous, amazing] [name of the article of clothing]. [They fit/It fits] perfectly, and I cannot wait to wear [them/it]. I am so thankful for your generosity during the holiday season.

Love and Peace,

____

Thank You for the Holiday Gift—Computer or Electronic Device

Dear ________________,

Wow! Thank you from the bottom of my heart! I totally love the [name of the item] you gave me. It is simply the greatest [name of holiday] gift ever. Now my fingertips can take me to all the places I want to go! Thank you for giving me the digital tools to help me explore the world! Happy New Year!

Love,

____

Thank You for the Holiday Gift—Game or Toy

Dear ________________,

I tore open the wrapping paper on your gift and had to blink my eyes! I have wanted the [name of toy/game] for so long! You have no idea! Thank you for making my holiday dreams come true. I hope you have a wonderful [name of holiday] and a Happy New Year!

Love,

____

Thank You for the Holiday Gift—Gift Card

Dear ______________,

Thank you for the gift card to [name of the store]! It's truly the perfect gift for me, and I can pick out exactly what I want. Thank you for your generosity and for always finding me the most amazing [name of the holiday] presents! Happy everything!

Peace,

____

Thank You for the Holiday Gift—Money

Dear ______________,

It was very exciting to open your [name of the holiday] card and find your generous gift! Thank you very much for thinking of the most amazing present ever and for remembering me on [name of the holiday]. I promise I will buy something wonderful or put it in my savings account for safekeeping! Happy Holidays!

Love,

____

Thank You for the Holiday Gift—Scarf or Mittens

Dear ______________,

I reached into your package to find something cozy! Thank you for the new [scarf/mittens] in my favorite shade of [name of color]. Now I will not only be warm but also be in style the whole winter. Sending you peace and joy throughout the holiday season and in the year to come.

Love,

____

Thank You for the Holiday Gift—Homemade Treats

Dear ______________,

I loved your present! I so appreciate the amazing [name of the holiday] [cookies/candy/treats]! With every single bite, I could feel all the holiday spirit you made them with. Thank you for filling me up with holiday cheer!

Your friend,

____

PS—I want to order more!

GRATEFUL GRINCH CHRISTMAS WISDOM

"And the Grinch, with his Grinch-feet ice-cold in the snow, stood puzzling and puzzling: 'How could it be so? It came without ribbons! It came without tags! It came without packages, boxes or bags!' And he puzzled three hours, till his puzzler was sore.

Then the Grinch thought of something he hadn't before!

'Maybe Christmas,' he thought, 'doesn't come from a store.

'Maybe Christmas . . . perhaps . . . means a little bit more!'"

—Dr. Seuss, *How the Grinch Stole Christmas*[49]

The Grateful Sage: Global Christmas Greetings

Arabic:	Milad Majid
Armenian:	Shnorhavor Amanor yev Surb Tznund
Chinese:	Shèngdàn jié kuàilè
English:	Merry Christmas
French:	Joyeux Noël
German:	Frohe Weihnachten
Gaelic:	Nollaig Shona Duit
Greek:	Kalá Christoúgenna
Hawaiian:	Mele Kalikimaka
Italian:	Buon Natale
Tagalog:	Maligayang Pasko
Polish:	Wesołych Świąt
Spanish:	Feliz Navidad

"May the force be with you."

—George Lucas, Star Wars[50]

GRATEFUL SAGE TIP

Make sure to write and send your holiday thank-you notes before you go back to school so you don't forget. If you can't write them all at once, write two a day until you get them finished! If you have a great holiday picture, you can send it through a stationery app with your electronic thank-you.

1. *Merriam-Webster Online*, s.v. "thank-you," accessed April 30, 2015, http://www.merriam-webster.com/dictionary/thank-you.

2. *Merriam-Webster Online*, s.v. "monogram," accessed April 30, 2015, http://www.merriam-webster.com/dictionary/monogram.

3. Albert Einstein, quoted in William Hermanns *Einstein and the Poet: In Search of the Cosmic Man* (Branden Press, 1983), 100.

4. *Merriam-Webster Online*, s.v. "integrity," accessed April 30, 2015, http://www.merriam-webster.com/dictionary/integrity.

5. Theodore Roosevelt, quoted on "Theodore Roosevelt Republican Club," accessed April 30, 2015, http://theodoreroosevteltclub.com/index.php/theodore-roosevelts-legacy/.

6. Ronald Reagan, "Remarks at the Ford Claycomo Assembly Plant in Kansas City, Missouri (speech given on April 11, 1984), accessed April 30, 2015, http://www.reagan.utexas.edu/archives/speeches/1984/41184a.htm.

7. Lisa Gaché, "Vote 'Yes' for Manners!" Beverly Hills Manners, accessed May 4, 2015, http://archive.constantcontact.com/fs054/1101650220060/archive/1102262592888.html.

8. *Merriam-Webster Online*, s.v. "honorable," accessed May 1, 2015, http://www.merriam-webster.com/dictionary/honorable.

9. *Merriam-Webster Online*, s.v. "compassion," accessed May 1, 2015, http://www.merriam-webster.com/dictionary/compassion.

10. Mother Teresa, "Mother Teresa Reflects on Working Toward Peace," Santa Clara University, accessed May 4, 2015, http://www.scu.edu/ethics/architects-of-peace/Teresa/essay.html.

11. *Merriam-Webster Online*, s.v. "sportsmanship," accessed May 1, 2015, http://www.merriam-webster.com/dictionary/sportsmanship.

12. Babe Ruth, quoted in "Babe Ruth," accessed May 1, 2015, http://www.baberuth.com/quotes/.

13. John Wooden, "Pyramid of Greatness," accessed May 1, 2015, http://www.coachwooden.com/pyramid-of-success.

14. John Wooden, quoted in "Pyramid of Success," accessed May 1, 2015, http://www.coachwooden.com/pyramid-of-success#Pyramid/1.

15. William Shakespeare, *King Henry VIII*, 1.4, accessed May 6, 2015, http://www.shakespeare-online.com/plays/henryviii_1_4.html.

16. Carl Lewis, quoted in David Barron "King Carl is now Coach Carl at UH," *Houston Chronicle*, last modified April 25, 2015, http://www.houstonchronicle.com/sports/college/article/King-Carl-is-now-Coach-Carl-at-UH-6224060.php.

17. Jesse Owens, quoted in "Sportsmanship Quotes," Institute for International Sport, accessed May 1, 2015, http://www.internationalsport.org/nsd/sportsmanship-quotes.cfm.

18. Dan O'Brien, quoted in "Dan O'Brien: On Greatness," The Good Men Project, last modified September 27, 2014, http://goodmenproject.com/sports-2/dan-obrien-on-greatness-mkdn/.

19. Summer Sanders, quoted in Ryan Griffith, "Inspirational Quotes from Famous Swimmers," Underwater Audio, accessed May 1, 2015, http://www.underwateraudio.com/blog/inspirational-quotes-from-famous-swimmers/.

20. *Merriam-Webster Online*, s.v. "civility," accessed May 1, 2015, http://www.merriam-webster.com/dictionary/civility.

21. *It's a Wonderful Life*, directed by Frank Capra (CA: Liberty Films, 1946).

22. Arnold Lobel, *Frog and Toad Are Friends* (New York City: HarperCollins, 2003).

23. J. K. Rowling, *Harry Potter and the Goblet of Fire* (New York City: Scholastic, 2002).
24. Taylor Swift, quoted on "Taylor Swift," IMDB, accessed May 1, 2015, http://www.imdb.com/name/nm2357847/bio.
25. Alice Walker, *In Search of Our Mothers' Gardens: Womanist Prose* (New York City: Mariner Books, 2003).
26. *Merriam-Webster Online*, s.v. "dignity," accessed May 1, 2015, http://www.merriam-webster.com/dictionary/dignity.
27. Katharine Hepburn, quoted in R. O. Bloch *What's it Take to Make a Man?* (San Francisco CA: Untreed Reads Publishing, 2012).
28. *Clueless*, directed by Amy Heckerling (Hollywood, CA: Paramount Pictures, 1995).
29. *Merriam-Webster Online*, s.v. "jealousy," accessed May 1, 2015, http://www.merriam-webster.com/dictionary/jealousy.
30. Steve Jobs, Commencement address to Stanford University, June 14, 2005, http://news.stanford.edu/news/2005/june15/jobs-061505.html.
31. Nelson Mandela, *Long Walk to Freedom: The Autobiography of Nelson Mandela* (New York City: Back Bay Books, 1995).
32. Will Durant, *The Story of Philosophy: The Lives and Opinions of the World's Greatest Philosophers* (New York City: Simon & Schuster, 1926).
33. Albert Einstein, quoted in Leopold Infeld *Quest: An Autobiography* (Providence, RI: American Mathematical Society, 2006).
34. *Merriam-Webster Online*, s.v. "jealousy," accessed May 1, 2015, http://www.merriam-webster.com/dictionary/respect.
35. *It's a Wonderful Life*, directed by Frank Capra (CA: Liberty Films, 1946).
36. Steve Jobs, quoted in Walter Isaacson "The Genius of Jobs," *New York Times*, October 29, 2011, http://www.nytimes.com/2011/10/30/opinion/sunday/steve-jobss-genius.html?_r=0.
37. William Shakespeare, *The Tempest*, 3.1, accessed May 1, 2015, http://shakespeare.mit.edu/tempest/tempest.3.1.html.

38. William Shakespeare, *Romeo and Juliet*, 2.2, accessed May 1, 2015, http://shakespeare.mit.edu/romeo_juliet/full.html.

39. William Shakespeare, *A Midsummer Night's Dream*, 1.1, accessed May 1, 2015, http://shakespeare.mit.edu/midsummer/full.html.

40. William Shakespeare, *The Tempest*, 3.1, accessed May 1, 2015, http://shakespeare.mit.edu/tempest/full.html.

41. William Shakespeare, *Hamlet*, 2.2, accessed May 1, 2015, http://shakespeare.mit.edu/hamlet/full.html.

42. William Shakespeare, *Macbeth*, 2.3, accessed May 1, 2015, http://shakespeare.mit.edu/macbeth/full.html.

43. *Merriam-Webster Online*, s.v. "determination," accessed May 1, 2015, http://www.merriam-webster.com/dictionary/determination.

44. Nelson Mandela, quoted in "Education for All," UN.org, accessed May 1, 2015, http://www.un.org/en/globalissues/briefingpapers/efa/quotes.shtml.

45. Joseph Campbell, *The Hero with a Thousand Faces* (Novato, CA: New World Library, 2008), 23.

46. Tom Fitzgerald, quoted in "Ask Dave: February 27–March 12, 2013," accessed May 1, 2015, https://d23.com/d23-presents-ask-dave-answers-to-questions-asked/.

47. Liv Tyler, *Modern Manners: Tools to Take You to the Top* (New York City: Potter Style, 2013).

48. *Merriam-Webster Online*, s.v. "peace," accessed May 1, 2015, http://www.merriam-webster.com/dictionary/peace.

49. Dr. Seuss, *How the Grinch Stole Christmas* (New York City: Random House Books, 1957).

50. *The Empire Strikes Back*, directed by Irvin Kershner, (San Francisco, CA: Lucasfilm Ltd, 1980).

About the Author

Author of the best-selling book *101 Ways to Say Thank You: Notes of Gratitude for all Occasions* (Sterling), Kelly Browne has written hundreds of thank-you notes in her personal, social, and professional life in motion pictures and television. Carrying endorsements from legendary stationery house Crane & Co., the global Protocol School of Washington, and the Etiquette & Leadership Institute, Ms. Browne has an extensive background in the social graces as a Southern California debutante and pageant winner and has appeared on dozens of media outlets worldwide. The recipient of numerous awards for her outstanding volunteer service in the community, including the prestigious US Presidential Volunteer Service Award, she was celebrated by the City of Los Angeles as an honoree for the Irish Woman of the Year.

Ms. Browne lives with her family in Los Angeles. To learn more, visit www.KellyBrowne.net.

0 26575 16416 9